Additional Particulars

by

Ed Simpson

NEW YORK HOLLYWOOD LONDON TORONTO

SAMUELFRENCH.COM

Copyright © 2008 by Ed Simpson

ALL RIGHTS RESERVED

CAUTION: Professionals and amateurs are hereby warned that *ADDITIONAL PARTICULARS* is subject to a royalty. It is fully protected under the copyright laws of the United States of America, the British Commonwealth, including Canada, and all other countries of the Copyright Union. All rights, including professional, amateur, motion picture, recitation, lecturing, public reading, radio broadcasting, television and the rights of translation into foreign languages are strictly reserved. In its present form the play is dedicated to the reading public only.

The amateur live stage performance rights to *ADDITIONAL PARTICULARS* are controlled exclusively by Samuel French, Inc., and royalty arrangements and licenses must be secured well in advance of presentation. PLEASE NOTE that amateur royalty fees are set upon application in accordance with your producing circumstances. When applying for a royalty quotation and license please give us the number of performances intended, dates of production, your seating capacity and admission fee. Royalties are payable one week before the opening performance of the play to Samuel French, Inc., at 45 W. 25th Street, New York, NY 10010.

Royalty of the required amount must be paid whether the play is presented for charity or gain and whether or not admission is charged.

Stock royalty quoted upon application to Samuel French, Inc.

For all other rights than those stipulated above, apply to: Samuel French, Inc., at 45 W. 25th Street, New York, NY 10010.

Particular emphasis is laid on the question of amateur or professional readings, permission and terms for which must be secured in writing from Samuel French, Inc.

Copying from this book in whole or in part is strictly forbidden by law, and the right of performance is not transferable.

Whenever the play is produced the following notice must appear on all programs, printing and advertising for the play: "Produced by special arrangement with Samuel French, Inc."

Due authorship credit must be given on all programs, printing and advertising for the play.

ISBN 978-0-573-66394-9   Printed in U.S.A.   #3754

No one shall commit or authorize any act or omission by which the copyright of, or the right to copyright, this play may be impaired.

No one shall make any changes in this play for the purpose of production.

Publication of this play does not imply availability for performance. Both amateurs and professionals considering a production are strongly advised in their own interests to apply to Samuel French, Inc., for written permission before starting rehearsals, advertising, or booking a theatre.

No part of this book may be reproduced, stored in a retrieval system, or transmitted in any form, by any means, now known or yet to be invented, including mechanical, electronic, photocopying, recording, videotaping, or otherwise, without the prior written permission of the publisher.

IMPORTANT BILLING AND CREDIT REQUIREMENTS

All producers of *ADDITIONAL PARTICULARS* *must* give credit to the Author of the Play in all programs distributed in connection with performances of the Play, and in all instances in which the title of the Play appears for the purposes of advertising, publicizing or otherwise exploiting the Play and/or a production. The name of the Author *must* appear on a separate line on which no other name appears, immediately following the title and *must* appear in size of type not less than fifty percent of the size of the title type.

ADDITIONAL PARTICULARS was first produced by The Occasional Theater (in association with Hothouse Peonies, and The West End) at Third Stage in Los Angeles, on May 13, 2000, under the direction of Michael Lilly, with setting and lights by James Henrickson, costumes by Sandy Gail, and stage management by Henry Lide, with the following cast:

GLENDA BALITSKI	Susan Mackin
WARREN GRIPPO	David Wells
KENNY HINKLE	Kirk Baily
RAYMOND FETTERMAN	Jack Kehler

ADDITIONAL PARTICULARS was developed at Keystone Repertory Theater, at Indiana University of Pennsylvania, Barbara Blackledge, Artistic Director.

CAST OF CHARACTERS

(in order of appearance)

GLENDA BALITSKI – Early 40's. A pleasant, plain, slightly plump clerk in the housewares department of Save-a-Bundle Discount Mart.

WARREN GRIPPO – Mid 40's. A conservatively dressed man of unflagging earnestness and good manners. He is the assistant manager at Save-a-Bundle Discount Mart.

KENNY HINKLE – Late 20's. A simple, pleasant, agreeable maintenance worker, content to just do his job.

RAYMOND FETTERMAN – Almost 47. Loquacious, dissatisfied maintenance worker desperately yearning for more from life.

For Michael and Brenda

Acknowledgments

The playwright is indebted to the army of artists and dear friends for their contributions to *Additional Particulars*.

Special thanks go to Michael Lilly; Brenda Lilly; the terrific original cast Susan Mackin, David Wells (the Warren and my pal), Jack Kehler, and Kirk Baily; my colleagues and students at Indiana University of Pennsylvania, especially Barbara Blackledge and Brian Jones; Keystone Repertory Theater; the Department of Theater at the University of North Carolina at Greensboro, especially John Gulley, Alan Cook, Carnessa Ottelin, Brandon Cardinal, and Erica Leiberman; David Tabish; John Martello; Marnie Andrews; Barry Bell; Michael Mahoney; Robin Kaver; Randy Newman; David Zarko of the Electric Theater Company; Hall Parrish and Stephen Gee of the Broach Theater; Tony Caselli, John Lepard, Emily Sutton-Smith and Christine Purchis of the Williamston Theater; Max; my great kids, Ben and Molly; and, finally, with love to Cyd.

Act I
"Glenda and Warren"

Synopsis of the Scene

It is early evening in the spring of this year.

Setting

The neatly furnished living room of Glenda Balitski's small apartment located in Randolphsburg, a small city in western Pennsylvania. There is a sofa with plastic Parsons tables on either end and a coffee table in front. On the Parsons tables are a pair of lamps. On the coffee table are a couple of magazines and, perhaps, a small figurine or two. A rocking chair is nearby as well as a TV on a small table. Along one wall is a small bookcase which holds a variety of photo albums and books, including a number of paperback romance novels. On top of the bookcase is a small "boom box." On one wall is a small, embroidered and framed sampler and a photograph of an older couple. In addition to the front door, there is a door to the kitchen and a doorway leading to a hall which leads to the bedroom and the bath. Whereas none of the furnishings are particularly new, it looks as if the occupant of the apartment has gone to great lengths to make it a home. In short, the room is the embodiment of "A place for everything, everything in its place."

Act II
"Kenny and Raymond"

Synopsis of the Scene

Lunchtime on the following Monday.

Setting

There is a doorway upstage leading from a corridor. Suspended from the ceiling are various steam pipes, water pipes, and power cords along with a couple of dusty light fixtures. Along one wall – a virtually hiding it – is a large stack of various sized boxes and crates. On the opposite wall are a couple of dingy safety posters, perhaps a few old typewritten memos taped to the wall, an old table, and a stack of old folding chairs in various states of repair.

(*SETTING:* Lights up to reveal **GLENDA**'s neat, orderly, precise little apartment.)

(*AT RISE:* **GLENDA** enters from the kitchen, carrying a bowl of Doritos. **GLENDA** is, like her apartment, neat and just a bit out of style. She sits on the sofa and places the Doritos on the coffee table. She smooths her skirt and, once she does this, looks about the room.)

(*She sighs contentedly, smiles, and then looks at the Dorito bowl for a moment as if trying to make a decision.*)

(*A pause – then she gets one Dorito and munches on it, wiping her mouth with a small napkin. While munching on the Dorito, she once again smoothes her skirt and looks about her little apartment. Short pause. Then...a polite knock on the door.* **GLENDA** *looks at the door for a moment.*)

GLENDA. That's odd.

(*Another polite knock and* **GLENDA** *crosses to the door and looks through the peephole.*)

Goodness.

(*She opens the door and there stands* **WARREN GRIPPO**, *a conservatively dressed man of unflagging earnestness and good manners. He wears a tie, a white, short-sleeved shirt, and a sports coat – all at least five years out of style.*)

Why, Mr. Grippo!

WARREN. Glenda – Hello.

GLENDA. *(very surprised)* Mr. *Grippo –*

WARREN. Warren.

GLENDA. Hmmm?

WARREN. Away from work it's Warren.

GLENDA. Oh. Well...fine – Warren.

WARREN. I apologize for dropping by without so much as a phone call –

GLENDA. That's alright. Would you like to come in?

WARREN. Well…if it's not inconvenient.

GLENDA. Not at all –

WARREN. Just for a moment. You're sure it's not inconvenient?

GLENDA. Not at all.

WARREN. Really?

GLENDA. Not at all.

WARREN. I was just on my way home. I could come back –

GLENDA. *(showing him in)* Come in, please.

(WARREN walks into the apartment and looks about.)

WARREN. Oh, well, this is lovely. This is very nice.

GLENDA. *(blushing)* Thank you.

WARREN. *(still looking around)* This is nice.

GLENDA. Won't you have a seat?

WARREN. Well, just for a minute.

(He sits.)

GLENDA. Doritos?

(beat)

WARREN. I'm sorry?

GLENDA. *(holding out the bowl)* They're the spicy kind. I hope you don't mind.

WARREN. Oh. *(He munches a chip.)* Ummmm. Tasty.

GLENDA. Would you like something to drink?

WARREN. *(starting to decline)* Oh –

GLENDA. I have soda, ice water –

WARREN. Well…ice water, thank you.

GLENDA. Or coffee?

WARREN. Water's fine.

GLENDA. Alrightie.

(She turns to go into kitchen.)

WARREN. Or...you know – maybe some soda after all.

GLENDA. Coming up.

(She starts to exit again when...)

WARREN. But...hmmm. Will that be too much trouble? I'll tell you...just ice water.

GLENDA. Soda's as easy as water, Warren.

WARREN. Oh? Well, then, soda it shall be.

(She goes to get the soda. He looks around, nervously adjusting his tie.)

Soda it shall be. *(beat)* Oh yes. This is lovely.

GLENDA. *(from the kitchen)* I moved here in February. Plunked down my security deposit and signed a lease for one year, thank you very much.

*(**GLENDA** comes out of kitchen with a can of soda and a glass with ice.)*

WARREN. Very cozy.

GLENDA. Well, a lot of planning and hard work went into this place, let me tell you. A lot of...well –

WARREN. Dreams?

(beat)

GLENDA. Why, yes...a lot of dreams and a lot of tender loving care.

WARREN. *(simultaneously)* – loving care. I can tell.

GLENDA. Before – you know – when I lived with my mother, when I was taking care of her before she...well – I used to dream of having my own place. And I knew just what it would look like. I knew where everything would go...there the stereo, there my bookshelf, there the television. Everything just so.

WARREN. *(simultaneously)* – just so, yes. Just so.

GLENDA. *(simply)* It's home. *(Beat. She hands him the drink.)* You did say soda, right?

WARREN. I did, yes. *(sips)* Oh my. This hits the spot. *(sips again)* Mmmm.

(A little awkward pause. Then…)

You mentioned your mother.

(She nods.)

Did she…?

(She nods.)

Recently?

GLENDA. Six months –

WARREN. Ah –

GLENDA. – two weeks, four days.

WARREN. I see. I'm sorry.

GLENDA. Thank you.

(beat)

WARREN. I mean, losing a parent. A loved one? Well… *(A pause. He crunches a chip. Then…)* The chips are delicious.

GLENDA. Aren't they?

(WARREN *eats another chip – which makes a loud crunch.)*

WARREN. *(rather embarrassed)* I didn't realize how hungry I was. I'm feeling a mite "peckish."

GLENDA. I do think they're addictive.

(She takes another chip.)

WARREN. Aren't they? One just leads to another and another –

GLENDA. *(simultaneously)* – and another and another –

(She munches her chip.)

WARREN. And before you know it, you've eaten a whole bag.

GLENDA. *(simultaneously)* – a whole bag. I know. We used to go through a couple of bags of Doritos every Saturday night. Honestly, we did.

WARREN. You and your mother?

(She nods.)

GLENDA. Can you believe it?

WARREN. *(munching)* They're addictive. You said it. They're addictive.

GLENDA. I've learned to control *that* little addiction, however.

WARREN. Really?

GLENDA. When I got my own place I said "That's it! I'm starting a new life, turning over a new leaf. I'll keep a bag around for special occasions but that is it!" And I've managed to stick to *that* little resolution, knock wood. *(She knocks on the plastic Parsons table. An embarrassed giggle.)* Whoops.

WARREN. Special occasions?

GLENDA. Yes, well…you know.

WARREN. Oh. *(a realization)* Oh! I am *so* sorry. I *am* imposing, aren't I?

GLENDA. No –

WARREN. *(He stands.)* I should have called. I should have called.

GLENDA. *(She stands.)* It's alright.

WARREN. Color *my* face red.

GLENDA. Please don't –

WARREN. I really should be going. I'm sorry. I just thought I'd drop by on my way home from the store.

GLENDA. But I'm glad you did…Warren. I am. Please – have a seat.

(He does so.)

It's a…pleasant surprise. I didn't even think you knew where I lived.

WARREN. I didn't really. Not until tonight. I mean, I knew you lived in this vicinity somewhere.

GLENDA. You did?

WARREN. *(nodding)* Uh-huh. I found myself following you one afternoon.

(beat)

GLENDA. You…you were following me?

WARREN. Hmmm? Oh! By accident. By accident.

GLENDA. Oh!

WARREN. Oh my…that sounded worse than I meant it to, didn't it?

(They share a nervous laugh.)

No – I simply meant that I discovered I was driving behind you one afternoon. And then you turned off and on I went! I honked and waved –

GLENDA. *(simultaneously)* – and waved! Why of course! That was *you?*

WARREN. *(raises his hand)* Guilty as charged. *(a little laugh)* I didn't think you recognized me.

GLENDA. I didn't.

WARREN. I didn't think so.

GLENDA. The glare from the sun. You know.

WARREN. It *is* awful, that time of day, isn't it – ?

GLENDA. *(simultaneously)* Isn't it?

(A rather awkward pause. **WARREN** *looks around the room as they both loudly crunch Doritos.* **WARREN***, looking about the room, finally points to one of the lamps on the end table next to the sofa.)*

WARREN. These are nice, aren't they?

GLENDA. I'm sorry?

WARREN. They're lovely. *(beat)* The lamps – ?

GLENDA. *(simultaneously)* Oh – the lamps! I love them!

WARREN. We had these on sale just after Easter.

GLENDA. *(simultaneously)* – after Easter. That's where I got them! And, with the 10% employee discount on top of the sale price –

WARREN. *(simultaneously)* – sale price, sure. It was an excellent value.

GLENDA. Absolutely.

WARREN. An out*stand*ing value. And they certainly fit the room.

GLENDA. Do you think so?

WARREN. One on either end of the sofa? Oh yes. That's nice. They – well, let's see – they *frame* the sofa somehow.

GLENDA. Well, a lamp on either side –

WARREN. *(simultaneously)* – on either side. Frames it. Sure.

GLENDA. It makes the room brighter, I think. More cheery.

WARREN. *(simultaneously)* – cheery. Hmmm. You know, you're right.

GLENDA. I like a bright room –

WARREN. *(agreeing)* A cheery room –

GLENDA. But not overhead lights.

WARREN. *(agreeing)* Oh no.

GLENDA. That's too much. It doesn't make as…

WARREN. Intimate?

(A beat. Finally…)

GLENDA. *(slightly embarrassed)* Yes. Yes, that's right…it doesn't make as – intimate a light. Too…well –

WARREN. Harsh?

GLENDA. Yes! Too harsh. With two table lights, you can… control the light.

WARREN. Sure. Sure you can.

(a slight pause)

GLENDA. But, that's neither here nor there.

WARREN. *(simultaneously)* – nor there. No. Neither here nor there. Anyway –

GLENDA. *(Simultaneously.)* Anyway.

(A slight beat. Then…)

WARREN. As I was saying earlier –

GLENDA. *(simultaneously)* – earlier. Yes – ?

WARREN. I knew the general direction you lived in. Knew that you lived somewhere on my way home but it wasn't until tonight that I knew exactly where you lived. You see, I had the occasion to go through your employment file this afternoon and took the liberty of noting your address.

GLENDA. *(worried)* My file? You went through my file? Mr. Grippo, is everything alright?

WARREN. What? *(beat as he realizes)* Oh! Oh, yes!

GLENDA. I mean, I just *thought*!

WARREN. Oh no –

GLENDA. Goodness! When you said you were looking at my file –

WARREN. Oh my *no*!

GLENDA. Not that I thought I had anything to worry about *but* –

WARREN. Think nothing of it. Put that thought *right* out of your mind. Do not concern yourself with *that*.

GLENDA. Whew!

WARREN. No. No problems at all. Just the opposite, as a matter of fact. The abso*lute* opposite.

(beat)

GLENDA. *Really?*

WARREN. In fact, you see, *that's* why I dropped by tonight. I wanted to phone from the store but as my message was of a somewhat…well – personal nature I thought it best not to tie up the line.

GLENDA. Personal?

(a beat)

WARREN. Well…strictly speaking personal *and* professional.

GLENDA. Personal and *professional?*

*(**WARREN** stands.)*

WARREN. Glenda Balitski, as Assistant Manager of the Valley Acre Mall location of Save-a-Bundle Discount Mart, I am pleased – *very* pleased – to inform you that you have been chosen…"Employee of the Month."

GLENDA. What?

WARREN. "Employee of the Month..."

GLENDA. *(simultaneously)* "...of the Month?" Oh my God!

WARREN. Congratulations –

GLENDA. Oh my God!

WARREN. *That's* why I came by tonight – !

GLENDA. Oh my God!

WARREN. I thought you'd want to know –

GLENDA. I can't believe this!

WARREN. I wanted to be the first to tell you –

GLENDA. *(impulsively hugging him)* Oh my God! Thank you!

WARREN. *(taken off guard)* Well...*(A delighted beat. Then...)* Thank *you* for your wonderful work in housewares, Glenda.

GLENDA. This is just unbelievable!

WARREN. Good work does not go unnoticed. You have excellent supervisor evaluations and...*(a slight pause)* Well, frankly, you maintain an attractive appearance if I might say so –

GLENDA. *(embarrassed)* Oh...

WARREN. And...well – your enthusiasm, Glenda – the obvious enthusiasm and pride you take as a member of the Save-a-Bundle team is exactly what we want to recognize.

GLENDA. I just do my job, really.

WARREN. And you do it well.

GLENDA. *(starts to cry)* Oh my.

WARREN. *(handing her his handkerchief)* Here. It's perfectly clean.

GLENDA. *(taking the handkerchief)* I'm sorry. It's just...I've never won anything before, not one thing in my entire life.

WARREN. Really? *(She nods.)* Well, that just startles me.

GLENDA. Mamma would've been *so* surprised. Whenever I got a little blue, you know, a little down –

WARREN. *(simultaneously)* – down. Right.

GLENDA. She would say "Glenny – "

WARREN. Glenny?

GLENDA. Uh-huh. That's what she called me. Glenny. "Glenny, your time may come...but don't count on it. There are winners... and then there is *you*."

WARREN. Oh... *no* –

GLENDA. Oh, but, see, Mamma didn't mean it in a *bad* way.

WARREN. She didn't?

GLENDA. Well, no. She thought people who lost were just as important as people who won. She always said "If there are no losers then what would be the point of trying to win?"

(beat)

WARREN. I see.

GLENDA. And, you know, really, when you look at it that way – she's right.

WARREN. You know, she is.

(A beat as she wipes her eyes again.)

GLENDA. I'm sorry.

WARREN. *(heading towards the kitchen)* Can I get you something to drink? A soda?

GLENDA. Water will be fine, thank you.

WARREN. A soda's no problem.

GLENDA. Just water, please.

WARREN. Water it is.

(He exits into the kitchen.)

GLENDA. *(softly, to herself)* Oh my goodness. *(to him)* How must I look to you right this very minute! Blubbering like a baby –

WARREN. *(from the kitchen)* Oh no. Oh no. I understand.

GLENDA. I've always been a bit...well – "weepy," mamma used to say.

*(**WARREN** re-enters.)*

When I'm happy I can just go all to pieces, I can.

(WARREN hands her a glass of water.)

WARREN. There, there.

GLENDA. I know it's just a silly award but still…

WARREN. Oh, but I understand. It's not silly. I know *exactly* how you feel. You see, I'm a past Employee of the Month myself.

GLENDA. Really?

WARREN. A two-time winner, in fact.

GLENDA. *(greatly impressed)* Two times?

WARREN. *(nodding)* June, 2006 and February, 2007 –

GLENDA. *(simultaneously)* – 07! Of course! I remember your picture next to the service desk!

WARREN. *(simultaneously)* – service desk!

GLENDA. *(simultaneously)* That was right after I began work –

WARREN. *(simultaneously)* – began work. Sure. That was I! February 2007. So if anyone knows how you feel, it is I.

GLENDA. Goodness. Then I…I suppose they'll put my picture right up there as well.

WARREN. Leo from shipping and receiving has a camera. He'll be in touch in a few days.

GLENDA. Oh.

(a slight pause)

WARREN. Is there a problem?

GLENDA. Hmmm? Oh. No. It's just that…I don't take a good picture.

WARREN. *(disbelieving)* No –

GLENDA. It's true. I don't. It never looks like me, I feel.

WARREN. *(still disbelieving)* No –

GLENDA. I always feel I look too heavy.

WARREN. Really?

GLENDA. *(She nods.)* Of course, I have had weight problems in the past.

WARREN. Now, see, that surprises me. Once again, I'm startled.

GLENDA. Really?

WARREN. You couldn't tell it now.

GLENDA. Really?

(He nods.)

Well, I take aerobics. Twice a week.

WARREN. That is excellent exercise. I have never participated myself but I have seen people…well, what would you call it? Aerobicing? – on video. *(beat)* We have a wide assortment of exercise videos in appliances.

GLENDA. *(Nodding)* I know. I…well – I gave myself one for Christmas last year. As a present.

WARREN. Really? Well… *(beat)* They make wonderful gifts, don't they?

GLENDA. Oh, they do. Still… *(A slight pause. Then, with a nervous laugh…)* I just don't take a good picture.

WARREN. Well… a photograph rarely captures what *kind* of person someone is.

(beat)

GLENDA. You know, I think that is so true.

(beat)

WARREN. "Employee of the Month –"

GLENDA. *(simultaneously)* "– of the Month!" *(an excited little giggle)* Goodness. I…I guess it just goes to show you that one person *can* make a difference.

WARREN. *That* was one of the things which attracted me to Save-a-Bundle in the first place.

GLENDA. Really?

WARREN. *(excitedly nodding)* I felt it was an organization in which I could very quickly make an impact.

GLENDA. Oh, and I think you have.

(a slight pause)

WARREN. Really?

GLENDA. Two employee of the month awards? Goodness, yes, I would say you have made a *definite* impact.

WARREN. *Really?*

(She nods enthusiastically.)

Well...it's the kind of organization that makes you want to contribute, you know.

GLENDA. I know, I know.

WARREN. I don't think you could find a better place to work. You see, I have an associate degree in business –

GLENDA. *(impressed)* Really?

WARREN. *(with great pride)* Allegheny County Community College. Yes, indeed. Anyway, when I received my degree, I interviewed with a number of companies and, let me tell you, Glenda, some pretty heavy hitters, too. Established national chains. But I was looking for a dynamic, growing company where I could step right in and make a difference. With Save-a-Bundle, I found – if you will – a professional home. I could tell from the first interview. You know, most people are interested in how a company can help them. Not me. I talked to Ted Crandall from the main office and I just asked, point blank "How can I help? What can I do to contribute?" Well, let me tell you, that surprised him. *That*, I think, he found refreshing, you know? He hesitated for a moment and you could see he was considering this proposition from all the angles. He had that look, you know? That look he gets when he's carefully looking at all the aspects. You know the look I'm talking about.

GLENDA. I've never actually seen him.

WARREN. Oh. Well...he has this look.

GLENDA. *(hanging on his every word)* So I've heard.

WARREN. Finally, he looked me right in the eyes, stuck out his hand, and said, "Well, to start out with, you can become a member of our *team* – " that's what he called it, Glenda, a team – "you can become a member of our team and within three years, you could advance right up the ladder to assistant manager." You know what I said?

GLENDA. *(hushed)* What?

WARREN. "Where do I sign?"

(She laughs.)

4 years, 2 employee of the month awards, 3 management trainee retreats later – here I am.

GLENDA. You certainly are! Goodness.

WARREN. Teamwork – that is the operative word.

GLENDA. And you know that's true. It *is* like a team, isn't it?

WARREN. Absolutely no question of it. And like any team, you have your MVP's –

*(He indicates **GLENDA**.)*

GLENDA. *(a little gasp)* Oh!

WARREN. "Employee of the Month."

GLENDA. *(a little shriek)* My God!

WARREN. And, of course, likewise, you have those who don't contribute to a winning season.

GLENDA. They warm the bench.

WARREN. *You* know what I'm talking about.

GLENDA. *(nodding)* I know.

WARREN. They never make the "Hall of Fame."

GLENDA. *That* is for sure –

WARREN. *(motioning to **GLENDA**)* They're never an All-Star –

GLENDA. Goodness, no –

WARREN. They should be traded!

GLENDA. Certainly –

WARREN. *Or...*cut from the team! Raymond Fetterman? In Maintenance – ?

GLENDA. *(simultaneously)* – in Maintenance!

WARREN. Yes!

GLENDA. Oh – you do *not* have to tell me about *him*.

WARREN. Very poor performance evaluations.

GLENDA. I should think *so.*

WARREN. *Extremely* poor.

GLENDA. How could they not be?

WARREN. His performance evaluations have plummeted. Management is none too pleased let me tell you.

GLENDA. Can you blame them?

WARREN. Mr. Becker asked me for my evaluation? I had no choice but to be candid. Shoot to outcome? I'm afraid our Mr. Fetterman is about to find his employment terminated.

GLENDA. *(a gasp)* Really?

WARREN. Well, there's only so much you can overlook. I mean, I like to think I have a pretty keen sense of humor but I *mean...*

GLENDA. I know. I do not think it's at all funny the way Raymond and those guys in Automotive imitate you.

(beat)

WARREN. You've seen that, then.

(She nods.)

GLENDA. It's really not funny.

WARREN. It's not.

GLENDA. It's not.

WARREN. It's really not. I mean, I like hilarity as much as anyone –

GLENDA. As do I, Warren –

WARREN. I can take a joke.

GLENDA. Me too –

WARREN. Hijinks have their place.

GLENDA. *(simultaneously)* – their place. Sure.

WARREN. Madcap antics – yes. Fine.

GLENDA. *(nodding)* Uh-huh –

WARREN. But on the job – ?

GLENDA. At work – ?

WARREN. It's inappropriate.

GLENDA. There's a time and a place –

WARREN. *(simultaneously)* – a place, yes – !

GLENDA. – for everything.

WARREN. *(simultaneously)* – everything, right. And what's sad – really, it's tragic – is that Raymond Fetterman is himself a past Employee of the Month –

GLENDA. *(simultaneously)* – of the *Month?*

WARREN. Yes!

GLENDA. *(shocked)* Raymond *Fette*man?

WARREN. *(nodding tragically)* April 2004.

GLENDA. *That* is hard to believe.

WARREN. How the mighty have fallen, huh?

GLENDA. But…well, I mean – what happened? How could someone go from –

WARREN. – Employee of the Month – ?

GLENDA. *(simultaneously)* – Employee of the Month – right – Employee of the Month to –

WARREN. *(simultaneously)* – to –

GLENDA. Exactly.

WARREN. I know. I know.

GLENDA. Why?

WARREN. Personal problems, he says.

GLENDA. Personal problems?

WARREN. *(simultaneously)* – problems, yes. Personal problems.

GLENDA. What kind of personal problems?

WARREN. *(with a shrug)* No one really knows. Very low self esteem I would imagine. You know.

GLENDA. Oh me.

(A slight pause as they contemplate this.)

WARREN. I mean, I am not unsympathetic to his circumstances. We all have…*things* in our lives. Events. *(a slight pause)* Obstacles.

GLENDA. *That* is true.

(**WARREN** *appears to be lost in his thoughts.*)

WARREN. Obstacles – to overcome…

(**GLENDA** *is, likewise, lost in thought.*)

GLENDA. We all have them.

WARREN. *(coming to)* Hmmm? Oh. That's right. Yes.

GLENDA. *(almost to herself)* I know *I* did.

WARREN. Really?

GLENDA. *(coming to)* Ummm…Oh. Yes.

WARREN. Well, then, you know what I mean.

GLENDA. Yes.

WARREN. *You* overcame them. For all the difficulty you moved beyond it.

GLENDA. I did.

WARREN. Life goes on –

GLENDA. It does.

WARREN. You can't dwell on past misfortunes –

GLENDA. It does no good –

WARREN. *That's* what I'm saying –

GLENDA. A positive attitude –

WARREN. Yes! Yes, a positive attitude –

GLENDA. It's the key to success.

WARREN. Mr. Raymond Fetterman in Maintenance and those tricksters in automotive would do well to heed *that* little bit of advice, believe you me.

GLENDA. I say, look on the bright side of life.

WARREN. *(fervently)* No whining around me. I have no time for negatives. I'm on the go! No looking back! The future is bright!

GLENDA. *(almost overwhelmed)* Goodness!

WARREN. I'll tell you something about myself. The secret of *my* success? I am a live wire, I'm happy to say. Shoot to outcome? I am an unapologetic go-getter, Glenda.

GLENDA. Oh, I can tell!

WARREN. You can? *(She nods. A pleased little pause, then...)* Well, I guess I like to think that's the most impressive thing I bring to the table so to speak. My enthusiasm –

GLENDA. Your dedication –

WARREN. My dedication, absolutely. Much like...well, if I might say so – much like yourself.

GLENDA. Oh. *(a beat)* Well – I guess I just love working there.

WARREN. It's a *fantastic* place to work, isn't it?

GLENDA. Uh-huh. I mean, I realize it's just retail –

WARREN. It's just retail –

GLENDA. But...I don't know – when you work there you feel...well, it's just great to be a part of something-

WARREN. *(simultaneously)* – something, yes!

GLENDA. Isn't it?

WARREN. That's all I've ever wanted, really.

GLENDA. To be a part of...something.

WARREN. Something. Yes. To be a part of something. *(beat)* I'll be candid, Glenda, there have been days...well, you know, you have those days –

GLENDA. Everybody does.

WARREN. Oh, sure, everybody does. You have those days when you get –

GLENDA. Discouraged?

WARREN. Oh, yes – discouraged by...by...

GLENDA. Life? *(beat)*

WARREN. Yes. Yes – *so* discouraged, when you feel as if...

GLENDA. I know.

WARREN. Well – frankly, on those days just walking through the front door –

GLENDA. *(with an excited gasp)* And seeing that little smiling bear?

WARREN. *(nodding)* Sammy Save-a-Bundle –

GLENDA. He is so *cute*!

WARREN. Oh, he's a delightful mascot –

GLENDA. *(with a laugh)* With that funny little *cap* – ?

WARREN. A very effective corporate symbol –

GLENDA. And that silly song he sings on the TV commercials – ?

WARREN. Instantly recognizable –

GLENDA. *(singing the jingle)* "Save a bundle, Ma! Save a bundle, Pa!"

WARREN. *(singing)* " – Pa! Save a bundle Goldilocks, too!"

GLENDA. *(singing)* " – Goldilocks, too!"

(They share a laugh.)

Goodness. *(beat)* You know, this may sound silly but... well.

WARREN. What?

GLENDA. Do you know when one of my favorite times of the day is?

WARREN. Just before the store opens – ?

GLENDA. *(simultaneously)* – store opens, yes! You too?

(WARREN sits on the opposite end of the sofa. Throughout the following exchange they inch toward the middle of the sofa.)

WARREN. Isn't it exciting?

GLENDA. The anticipation –

WARREN. The promise! What will the day hold?

GLENDA. The feeling that you are moving forward –

WARREN. *(simultaneously)* – forward, yes, moving forward. Retail is always changing –

GLENDA. *(simultaneously)* – changing. Everyday is a new challenge.

WARREN. It's new –

GLENDA. You don't know what's going to happen –

WARREN. And you wonder –

GLENDA. "Am I up to it?"

WARREN. Because you know there are going to be people –

GLENDA. Customers –

WARREN. Customers, absolutely, demanding the best value for their dollar.

GLENDA. Well, why not? They've worked for it –

WARREN. It's their money –

GLENDA. The very best value –

WARREN. We provide it!

GLENDA. It's a service!

WARREN. Oh! And the delight on their faces when they find a value?

GLENDA. A bargain?

WARREN. It doesn't get any better than that!

GLENDA. It doesn't!

WARREN. It doesn't!

(They are now sitting very close to each other. A slight pause as they look into each others excited faces. Finally...)

GLENDA. Goodness! *(a rather breathless beat...)* Doritos?

(Pause as they try to regain their composure. Then...)

WARREN. Thank you, Glenda.

(He sits, she sits, and they both munch a Dorito. Finally...)

Perhaps a bit more soda?

GLENDA. *(simultaneously)* – soda, sure.

(She exits into the kitchen. **WARREN** *stands and walks about, sipping his soda.)*

WARREN. *(to himself.)* Oh, my.

*(***WARREN*** checks his breath, pulls out a roll of mints, pops one into his mouth and, rather loudly, sucks on it while closely looking at the sampler. He absently pops yet another two or three mints into his mouth. At this,* **GLENDA** *re-enters carrying a soda in one hand and awkwardly holding some ice in the other.)*

GLENDA. Ice?

WARREN. Hmmm?

GLENDA. *(holding up the ice)* A freshener?

WARREN. Oh. Ummm....

(For a moment he doesn't quite know what to do. Should he swallow the mint, ditch it, or crunch it? For her part, the ice is obviously making **GLENDA** *uncomfortable. Finally* **WARREN** *crunches loudly, surprising her. He laughs nervously and extends his glass.)*

Thank you.

(She dumps the ice in his glass.)

GLENDA. Here you are.

(He nods. A slightly awkward pause. Finally, he notices her little book-shelf and walks over to it.)

WARREN. My. Quite a library.

GLENDA. *(simply)* I love to read.

WARREN. Give me a comfortable chair and an good book and I'm....

(A brief pause as he searches for the right word.)

GLENDA. Happy?

WARREN. Well...content, really.

GLENDA. Content! Oh, yes.

(He pulls out one of the books – a paperback romance novel with a muscular, bare-chested man embracing a woman on the cover.)

WARREN. *(a bit surprised)* Oh. *(A beat. As he recovers:)* Yes. Well...you know, these are very popular at the store.

GLENDA. *(trying to cover)* Really?

WARREN. Historical romances? Oh, my yes. We sell an awful lot of these at checkout.

GLENDA. *(embarrassed)* I'm...well, I fancy myself a history buff, actually. I read them for the history.

WARREN. Really?

GLENDA. That's what I find fascinating about these books, really. The history.

WARREN. *(simultaneously)* – history. I see.

GLENDA. Yes. The people back in those days, those...historical days. They were just so interesting, I find.

WARREN. And the *artwork*...

GLENDA. Sorry?

WARREN. The artwork on the cover? It's very effective. From a marketing perspective.

GLENDA. Oh. Well...Yes. Yes.

WARREN. *(searching for the right word)* Very...well, very –

GLENDA. Ummm...

WARREN. Robust?

GLENDA. Oh. Sorry – what?

WARREN. Robust.

GLENDA. Robust. Of course.

*(A embarrassed little pause during which **GLENDA** puts the book back on the shelf and **WARREN** unconsciously hikes up his pants a notch. Finally...)*

WARREN. Yes...the great outdoors.

GLENDA. Hmmm?

WARREN. Like...mmmm –

(He points toward the book.)

GLENDA. Oh.

WARREN. I'm something of an outdoorsman, myself, you know?

GLENDA. Really?

WARREN. *(nodding)* It's a...bit of a passion of mine, really.

GLENDA. Are you a camper?

(beat)

WARREN. Am I...?

GLENDA. Do you camp?

WARREN. Well...in truth, not often. I *did* go one time. In a little tent. *(a slight pause)* It rained. The whole time.

GLENDA. Oh.

WARREN. *(a slight pause)* But the woods, you know? And the trails?

GLENDA. So you're a hiker?

(beat)

WARREN. Hmmm? Oh. Well…I do like a good walk in the woods, that is for sure.

GLENDA. Isn't it wonderful? So calm. So peaceful.

WARREN. Unfortunately, a hectic work schedule and allergies make those occasions rare.

GLENDA. Oh dear. Allergies?

WARREN. *(nodding)* I'm allergic to trees, actually.

GLENDA. Oh no! Trees?

WARREN. Yes.

GLENDA. But they're everywhere!

WARREN. *(simultaneously)* – everywhere. Yes.

GLENDA. I mean, *everywhere!*

WARREN. *(simultaneously)* Everywhere. *(with a sigh)* I know.

GLENDA. You poor thing. How…how –

WARREN. Sad?

GLENDA. Well…yes but…well, really, I was going to say how…ironic.

(beat)

WARREN. Ironic?

GLENDA. That you're an outdoorsman who's allergic to trees. It's very ironic. *(a beat) And* sad, too, of course.

WARREN. Oh. Yes. It *is* isn't it?

GLENDA. *(simultaneously)* So you really can't be outdoors very much, can you.

WARREN. Truthfully? No. But…well, I suppose I'm an outdoorsman in spirit.

GLENDA. I see. *(beat)*

WARREN. That really sounds rather foolish, doesn't it?

GLENDA. Oh no – not at all. I understand *completely.* I'm many things in spirit.

WARREN. Really?

GLENDA. *Many* things. I mean, I had to be.

WARREN. *Really?*

GLENDA. Well, it was difficult for me to be too much in *reality* while Mamma was alive so… *(beat)*

WARREN. I don't understand.

GLENDA. You see, my mother was…you know. She was just one of those people who could not be left alone for very long so I had to…well.

WARREN. Oh, I see. I see. Yes. Invalid, was she?

GLENDA. Hmmm? Oh, no. No. Not at all. Not really. Although… *(Beat. Then, with a little laugh…)* Well…yes. I guess. In a way. You see, she had needs.

WARREN. Oh.

GLENDA. Many, *many* needs –

WARREN. Ah!

GLENDA. And it fell to me to provide them.

WARREN. *(simultaneously)* – provide them. Uh-huh. I see. Goodness.

GLENDA. It was my responsibility. Ever since I was very small.

(beat)

WARREN. No.

GLENDA. Maybe 13 or so. Yes.

WARREN. 13 or so?

GLENDA. *(simultaneously)* – or so. I know.

WARREN. But why did she – ?

GLENDA. I don't know. I guess Mamma was just one of those people, you know – ?

WARREN. Well –

GLENDA. One of those people who find every day so very frightening and so very difficult that it's all they can do just to grumble their way through the day.

WARREN. Oh. Well, yes. I see.

GLENDA. She needed all the help she could get so I had to be there for her. After school. Nights and weekends.

Most of the time. *(beat) All* the time, really. It used to make me *so* mad.

WARREN. I would think!

GLENDA. I know that makes me sound very selfish –

WARREN. Oh, no –

GLENDA. But I was young –

WARREN. 13 or so! I mean, really – ! You must've felt like a prisoner –

GLENDA. *(simultaneously)* – a prisoner. I did. Sometimes, I did, yes. But…*(beat)* Well, she was my mother.

WARREN. I suppose she was.

GLENDA. She was. And I don't believe she chose to live the way she did. She certainly got no pleasure out of it. And I really do think that in her very peculiar way she appreciated the way I was always there for her. And, really, you know, I suppose it made feel – well, needed… valuable, I guess. And it was hard for me, really, when she died. However – and, oh, goodness, I hate feeling this way but – when she finally… *(beat)* I felt so…

(pause)

WARREN. I see.

GLENDA. Anyway, throughout all of that, even as a child, you see, I was…aware –

WARREN. Aware?

GLENDA. Of the world, yes, and aware, somehow, that if I wanted to live I had to somehow remain apart –

WARREN. *(simultaneously)* – apart, yes, I see –

GLENDA. You see? I had to remain apart from her tiny, tiny world. *(beat)* So, I guess you could say that at least, in spirit –

WARREN. *(simultaneously)* – in spirit –

GLENDA. I had to –

WARREN. I see –

GLENDA. Live. Yes. That's why I knew exactly what my first home away from hers would look like. That's why being honored as "Employee of the Month –

WARREN. *(simultaneously)* " – of the Month -"

GLENDA. – is *literally* a dream come true. I have been and am now *many* things in spirit. And that is why I understand *completely.*

WARREN. I see.

GLENDA. *(nodding)* My world is much bigger than it appears.

WARREN. It is?

GLENDA. Much bigger. *(Beat. With a smile.)* At least… "in spirit."

WARREN. I see. *(A beat then…)* Well –

GLENDA. *(simultaneously)* Well – *(An awkward little pause. Then…)*

WARREN. *(standing)* I must be going.

GLENDA. *(disappointed)* Oh –

WARREN. I should have phoned first.

GLENDA. *(standing)* But –

WARREN. *(crossing toward the door)* Once again, my sincerest congratulations.

GLENDA. *(following him)* Thank you but –

WARREN. No, I'm keeping you from –

GLENDA. What?

WARREN. Well, I mean, the Doritos –

GLENDA. What?

WARREN. Only for "special occasions – "

GLENDA. Huh? Oh –

WARREN. You were obviously expecting a guest.

GLENDA. Oh no.

WARREN. A special someone – ?

GLENDA. There's no one!

(a slight pause)

WARREN. Oh.

GLENDA. I mean…well. Not…not tonight.

WARREN. I see –

GLENDA. Or any other night either.

(beat)

WARREN. Oh. I see. *(a slight pause)* But the… *(pointing the Doritos)* special occasion?

GLENDA. *(with a shrug)* I guess just making it through the week.

(A pause as they look at each other, uncertain of what to do next. Then…)

WARREN. Well…*that* can certainly be a special occasion.

GLENDA. It can, yes.

WARREN. You don't have to tell *me* –

GLENDA. I'll bet.

WARREN. After the week *I've* had? *(He wipes imaginary sweat from his brow.)* Whew.

GLENDA. *(delighted)* Really?

WARREN. *(He again wipes his brow.)* Whew.

(GLENDA giggles, captivated. A beat then…)

I mean, as you might imagine, it takes a tremendous amount of effort to help the Save-a-Bundle team pass along the very best in savings to our customers.

GLENDA. I can only imagine.

WARREN. The pressure's pretty intense for those of us in management, believe you me.

GLENDA. I'll bet.

WARREN. Pretty darn intense, if you must know. I mean, frankly, the assistant manager is vital, Glenda – vital to the smooth operation of any retail outlet.

GLENDA. Really?

WARREN. You have so many things to do. So many responsibilities.

GLENDA. It must be very difficult.

WARREN. You're on your feet all the time, moving about the store, checking all aspects of the operation. I maintain a list, Glenda, a list and, as I walk through the store, I note my thoughts, my observations, my reflections, my suggestions for improving the operation of the store. I like to think it encapsulates my retail philosophy.

GLENDA. Goodness!

WARREN. Of course, Mr. Becker is rather reticent to take advantage of my insights but...well. *(a beat)* I maintain my list, Glenda, because you have to make sure everything is just so, you know? Just so!

GLENDA. *(simultaneously)* – just so. Uh-huh.

WARREN. It has to be just so! If not, who do you think gets the blame?

(beat.)

GLENDA. You?

WARREN. The buck stops here. Right here. *(beat)* The pressure is enormous – it's overwhelming. The day to day operations are one thing. But then when you have the unexpected like the incident Tuesday with the slushy machine at the snack bar –

GLENDA. *(with a laugh)* That was such a mess – !

WARREN. Not my fault! Strictly speaking it was not my fault.

GLENDA. Oh. Well, I know –

WARREN. All I wanted was to see how they make those... tiny, little bubbles! I had just crawled behind the slushy machine when...blooie!

GLENDA. It was so loud!

WARREN. It was everywhere! I've never heard of a slushy machine doing that before!

GLENDA. Me neither –

WARREN. If they don't want you touching certain buttons and levers behind the machine they need to put up a sign!

GLENDA. It was an accident!

WARREN. Try telling that to Mr. Becker when you're

standing in his office covered in blueberry slushy! I mean, you know what he's like.

GLENDA. Actually he never comes to housewares.

WARREN. He was not happy. Not happy at all. It was a nightmare. *(A big sigh.* **WARREN** *has succeeded in bringing himself down.)* I don't know what I was thinking. This is not the time for those sort of shenanigans. All that talk about cutbacks in middle-management? Well, that little item has moved well past the rumor stage. *Well* past.

GLENDA. Oh.

(a slight pause)

WARREN. If I didn't have my job, I would not have…I can't…I can't

GLENDA. Do you really think Mr. Becker would –

WARREN. The bottom line is the bottom line.

GLENDA. Oh, but you've been Employee of the Month – twice!

WARREN. *(simultaneously)* – twice, yes.

GLENDA. You're vital! You just said it yourself – you're vital!

WARREN. Well –

GLENDA. You're essential!

WARREN. I'm afraid that in retail it's "what have you done for me lately?

GLENDA. But your loyalty to Save-a-Bundle –

WARREN. I know –

GLENDA. Your dedication –

WARREN. *(simultaneously)* – dedication. I know, I know –

GLENDA. You've proven that! It must count for something. Right? I'm sure Mr. Becker and upper management recognize that.

WARREN. *(shrugging)* Well… *(beat)* You can't question my devotion to the company philosophy.

GLENDA. Teamwork. Right?

WARREN. Oh, it's great being part of the team, isn't it?

GLENDA. And your enthusiasm – !

WARREN. You can't question my enthusiasm.

GLENDA. Your enthusiasm is unquestioned.

WARREN. Well, I've said it before, I'll say it again – I just think it's a wonderful place to work.

GLENDA. It is.

WARREN. Competitive salary. Potential for advancement. *(beat) Excellent* benefits package –

GLENDA. *(nodding)* The dental plan –

WARREN. Major medical, eye care, right?

GLENDA. Oh yes! Yes, indeed. Those things are important.

WARREN. Oh, absolutely. *(a pause. Then…)* Thank you.

GLENDA. Oh, well…

WARREN. I suppose it's just been one of those weeks. You know.

GLENDA. We all have them.

WARREN. We all do. *(a pause as* **WARREN** *sighs)* The thing is, I've worked so *hard* to be a part of the Save-a-Bundle team because I've never had…and, you see, my job is important to me – very, very important…*(beat)* I mean, it's a career, really, it's more than a job, it's a career, a way of life, a way of being – you know? – a way of being a part – right? – a part of something bigger and better than yourself.

(Pause as **GLENDA** *sits beside* **WARREN**. *Then…)*

GLENDA. Well, I think you're fine. You don't need to be a part of something bigger. *(beat)* That's what I think. Really.

(A pause. They are very close to each other. Then…)

WARREN. Glenda, I…

GLENDA. Yes, Warren?

(a beat)

WARREN. *(standing)* I'm sorry. I must apologize –

GLENDA. What?

WARREN. *(walks away, agitated)* I came here tonight under false pretenses. I…I have been less than candid with you.

GLENDA. Less than candid – ?

WARREN. *(simultaneously)* – candid, yes, less than candid.

GLENDA. *(simultaneously)* – candid. Oh. I see.

WARREN. I must be frank, Glenda. The Employee of the Month –

GLENDA. *(simultaneously)* – of the Month – ?

WARREN. Yes – the Employee of the Month award –

GLENDA. Oh no!

WARREN. What?

GLENDA. I didn't get it? I'm really not Employee of the Month?

WARREN. Oh! No! No!

GLENDA. I'm *not*?

WARREN. No, no – I mean…yes! Yes, you *are* –

GLENDA. I am?

WARREN. You are! You are, indeed. Rest assured. Your Employee of the Month award is richly deserved.

GLENDA. Really?

WARREN. *Richly* deserved.

GLENDA. But…you just said you had not been candid –

WARREN. *(simultaneously)* – candid, no. No, I haven't. *(beat)* To put a point to it, there are… well – additional particulars…

GLENDA. Additional particulars?

WARREN. *(simultaneously)* – particulars, yes – additional particulars that I had hoped to discuss with you.

GLENDA. What kind of particulars, Warren?

WARREN. Particulars of a…well – particular *kind.*

(**GLENDA** *is confused. Beat.*)

Particulars of a *personal* nature. Particulars which could have…ramifications.

GLENDA. *(still confused)* Particulars which could have – ?

WARREN. – ramifications, yes. *(beat)*

GLENDA. I'm very confused.

WARREN. It's very complicated. You see, there are policies –

GLENDA. Policies. I see.

WARREN. Yes – company policies which define what is acceptable and what is unacceptable and what is appropriate and what is inappropriate –

GLENDA. *(simultaneously)* – inappropriate – uh-huh.

WARREN. Absolutely – regarding the nature of…well – *(beat)* personal conduct between co-workers –

GLENDA. Ohhhh…

WARREN. And, indeed, we are, in point of fact –

GLENDA. *(nodding)* Co-workers –

WARREN. Yes! I mean, Glenda, we…we work…

GLENDA. Together –

WARREN. Together – absolutely! Strictly speaking, I am your supervisor and company policy is very clear regarding what might be construed as…well, pardon me but regarding what might be construed as…you know. *(beat)* Harassment?

GLENDA. Oh. Ohhh.

WARREN. *(tumbling out)* Yes! And which is *strictly* defined as the inappropriate introduction of certain…activities of an unwanted, personal or…intimate nature into relationships of unequal power such as the one you and I enjoy at Save-a-Bundle. And herein lies my difficulty. As part and parcel of my professional obligations I have closely observed your out*standing* work in housewares and… for the longest time – and in spite of my loyalties to a company policy which, after all, exists for the protection of *all* – I have wished that a…well – friendship could be forged between us which would transcend our professional relationship.

(A pause. Finally…)

GLENDA. Oh.

WARREN. I'm sorry – I've put you in an awkward position –

GLENDA. No –

WARREN. What must you think of me?

GLENDA. Nothing!

WARREN. *(Disappointed.)* What?

GLENDA. No! I mean – I... *(A Beat. To recover.)* Warren, I could never, ever think ill of you in *any* way at *any* time for *any* reason whatsoever. None. I hold you in the highest – the abso*lute* highest regard – not only as a supervisor but as a person whom I could...could –

WARREN. *(simultaneously)* – could? Yes?

GLENDA. Well, if I understand you correctly, the company policies pertain to activities which are... undesired.

WARREN. *(simultaneously)* – undesired. Yes. Strictly speaking, undesired.

GLENDA. Well...you don't have to worry about the ramifications – because your actions are certainly not undesired.

(beat)

WARREN. Oh.

GLENDA. You see, I have...observed you as well, Warren.

WARREN. What?

GLENDA. I suppose I'd always felt that, despite the fact that I am labor and you are management that we were, perhaps, kindred spirits.

(beat)

WARREN. You were aware of me? *(She nods.)* Goodness.

GLENDA. I hope you don't mind.

WARREN. Oh no! It's just that to my knowledge I've never been...well...

GLENDA. Admired?

WARREN. Well...yes. I guess...admired from afar.

GLENDA. *(simultaneously)* – from afar.

WARREN. Yes.

(They look at each other a moment. Finally, with a polite awkwardness, **WARREN** *leans over and gives* **GLENDA** *kiss. When they finish the kiss, they pull back, smiling, not knowing what to do next but comfortable with that. A pause. Finally…)*

GLENDA. Warren?

WARREN. Yes?

GLENDA. There's something I've been…well – meaning to ask.

WARREN. *(simultaneously)* – meaning to ask? Uh-huh?

(beat)

GLENDA. Have you noticed –

WARREN. *(simultaneously)* – noticed? Yes. Yes, I have.

GLENDA. How often we–

WARREN. *(simultaneously)* – we…?

(He motions back and forth between them.)

GLENDA. Yes!

WARREN. I know. Sorry, I –

GLENDA. Oh no – no! It's perfectly alright. Don't you see? Warren, it's almost as if we were…

WARREN. Simpatico?

GLENDA. *(nodding)* Of the same mind –

WARREN. On the same wave-length –

GLENDA. *(simultaneously)* – wave-length! Yes –

WARREN. *(simultaneously)* Yes. As if we *knew* –

GLENDA. As if we *felt* –

WARREN. Yes! Yes, as if we felt just what the other is feeling.

GLENDA. *(simultaneously)* – feeling. I know!

WARREN. Shared feelings.

GLENDA. *(simultaneously)* – feelings.

WARREN. Shared…desires.

GLENDA. *(simultaneously)* – desires, yes. Shared desires.

WARREN. Of one mind.

GLENDA. Of one heart. Of one...

WARREN. *(simultaneously)* One...

(beat)

GLENDA. One.

WARREN. Yes. Yes. One.

(A long pause as they look at each other. Finally...)

I have *seldom* –

GLENDA. I understand.

WARREN. I mean, *very* seldom.

GLENDA. It's alright.

WARREN. I suppose I'm just not the sort of person women often find –

GLENDA. Oh, no –

WARREN. No. Really!

GLENDA. Well...now *that* startles *me.*

WARREN. Really? It does? Well.

(beat)

GLENDA. *(Handing him the basket of chips.)* Dorito – for a special occasion?

WARREN. A special occasion. Yes. That would be nice.

(They sit side by side, munching and contentedly holding hands. Then...)

GLENDA. *(Softly singing...)* "Save a bundle Ma, save a bundle Pa – "

WARREN. *(simultaneously)* " – a bundle Pa, save a bundle Goldilocks, too."

GLENDA. *(simultaneously)* " – save a bundle Goldilocks too."

(They chuckle appreciatively as they continue to sit. A pause. Then, as one, they each loudly munch a Dorito and, pondering their own happy thoughts, simultaneously chew as the lights fade out.)

End of Part I

(**SETTING:** *A dingy storage room in the basement Sav-a-Bundle Discount Mart. A very large stack of cardboard boxes is on one side of the room.*)

(**AT RISE:** **KENNY** *enters, carrying a lunch box. He finds a place to sit and a crate to use as a little table. Once seated,* **KENNY** *opens his lunch box and happily unpacks his lunch.*)

(*A beat then* **RAYMOND** *appears, quickly walking past the door, looking around with a certain amount of confusion as he goes. Another beat. And then* **RAY** *reappears in the door. He stands for a moment, holding a rumpled lunch bag in one hand, a can of soda in the other, wearing a confused frown. He appears to be a bit preoccupied.*)

(**KENNY**, *who is happily chewing on a sandwich, sees* **RAY**.)

KENNY. Raymond?

(**RAYMOND** *"comes to" and* **KENNY** *cheerfully waves his sandwich at him…a beat then…*)

RAYMOND. *(holding up the can of soda)* When these become 60 cents?

KENNY. What?

RAYMOND. They were 55 now they're 60.

KENNY. *(shaking his head and chewing)* Jeez-o-beezus.

RAYMOND. You know why, don't you?

KENNY. Suits?

RAYMOND. Suits.

KENNY. *(shaking his head again)* Jeez-o-beezus –

RAYMOND. Trying to soak us a extra nickel.

KENNY. Yeah.

RAYMOND. You believe those guys?

KENNY. Those guys.

RAYMOND. Those guys.

KENNY. Boy.

(RAY sits heavily.)

RAYMOND. Don't even get me started on *those* guys.

(With a grunt as he pulls a sandwich from his bag.)

Suits. I mean, Grippo, O.K.?

(A cursory inspection of his sandwich and he takes a bite.)

Grippo –

KENNY. Yeah?

RAYMOND. Cracks me up. Carrying around that little notebook a his, watching you do things, writing down these little items, these little reports like he's some kinda big shot. Huh? *(He laughs.)* Am I right, Kenny?

KENNY. *(agreeing)* He just does what Mr. Becker tells him.

RAYMOND. Come on! *Grippo? (laughs)* I mean, it's really kinda sweet. He's just this little suit, you know?

KENNY. Yeah –

RAYMOND. And he's supposed to be the boss of *me*? He's supposed to tell *me* what to do? *(Laughs as he opens his soda.)* Kenny, I been a valued employee 10 years almost. 10 *years*.

KENNY. Yeah. 10 years. Boy –

RAYMOND. If anybody should be ordering others around it should be Raymond Fetterman, Kenny.

(RAYMOND takes a gulp of his soda.)

KENNY. *(snickering)* Yeah, right –

RAYMOND. Why not?

KENNY. You a suit – Jeez-o-beezus –

RAYMOND. Hey – I was Employee of the Month that one time!

(KENNY is stunned.)

KENNY. *You?*

RAYMOND. Yeah.

KENNY. *(laughing)* You?

RAYMOND. April 2004. Before you got here.

(KENNY continues to snicker.)

What?

KENNY. *(with a laugh)* Nothing.

RAYMOND. Got my picture hung up behind the service desk and this certificate for a Whopper and fry over at Burger King. Sure.

KENNY. Boy, that's great –

RAYMOND. Hey – I wanna tell you what – *(takes a bite of his sandwich)* If Grippo didn't go to college that year and wear a tie all the time and kiss the boss's ass, he'd be taking orders from me. I'd be the one telling *him* to do this and that and one thing or another. So don't get me started on Grippo.

KENNY. I won't.

(A beat as RAY chews. Then...)

RAYMOND. I mean, he sends us down here for some damn reason or other – doesn't even tell us *why?* This make sense to *you?*

KENNY. I don't know. He told *me.*

(He takes a bite of his sandwich.)

RAYMOND. *You?* Grippo told *you* what he wanted us to do?

(KENNY nods.)

When?

KENNY. When you went to the crapper.

RAYMOND. When I went to the *crapper?*

(KENNY nods and chews.)

So when you two get to be such good friends?

KENNY. We're not friends –

RAYMOND. *(teasing)* What'd he – put *you* in charge?

KENNY. *(snickering)* No –

RAYMOND. You supposed to tell *me* what to do?

KENNY. No –

RAYMOND. You supposed to be the boss of *me*, Kenny, huh? That it?

KENNY. *(laughing)* Jeez-o-beezus –

RAYMOND. Hey, O.K. Fine. Now I understand. *(takes a bite of sandwich)* So…what're we supposed to do, boss?

KENNY. *(smiling)* We just gotta move the boxes, Ray. That's all.

RAYMOND. What…? *Those* boxes?

(KENNY nods.)

Where we supposed to move 'em?

KENNY. *(pointing to the opposite wall)* Over there.

(Beat. As RAY looks. Then…)

RAYMOND. From one side to the *other*?

KENNY. That's what he said.

RAYMOND. From here to there?

(KENNY nods.)

Back and *forth*?

(KENNY nods. RAY considers this. Then…)

Grippo happen to tell you *why*?

KENNY. He's our boss, Raymond. He doesn't have to tell us why.

RAYMOND. I got a right to know why I'm moving these things.

KENNY. *(with a laugh)* No you don't.

RAYMOND. What – I don't got rights now just cause the suits decide a buncha boxes in storage for who knows how long gotta be moved about?

(KENNY Considers this. Then…)

KENNY. I don't know.

RAYMOND. A man needs a reason, Kenny. That's all I'm

saying. A man doesn't have a reason – ?

KENNY. Yeah.

RAYMOND. Those guys.

KENNY. Those guys. *(They eat for a moment. Then...)* So... how you doin', Ray?

*(No answer as **RAY** continues to brood.)*

Ray?

RAYMOND. *(looking up)* Huh?

KENNY. How you doin'?

RAYMOND. Oh. *(with a grunt)* I were any better they'd haveta lock me up and do tests.

(taking a bite)

I wanna tell you *what...*

KENNY. What's that?

*(Beat. **RAYMOND** has no answer. Then, musing...)*

RAYMOND. I don't know – maybe I'll get me a truck, you know? And one of those things.

KENNY. What?

RAYMOND. You know – a top?

KENNY. Oh –

RAYMOND. Like a camper?

KENNY. A camper.

RAYMOND. A camper top, yeah.

KENNY. Yeah.

RAYMOND. Maybe a trailer. Get one of those camping trailers with a bed and a little table and a refrigerator and a crapper. One of those little microwaves.

KENNY. That's campin'?

RAYMOND. That's *livin'*, pal. That's livin' it *up*, that's what *that* is.

KENNY. They got T.V.'s with some of them. Cable.

RAYMOND. Cable. Sure. I know this guy's got one of those satellite dishes hooked up to his RV. You can see shows from Australia twenty four hours a day.

KENNY. Australia?

RAYMOND. South America, too – sure. Europe. Las Vegas, Nevada. All over the world. Any kinda show you want.

KENNY. *(considering the miracle of this)* Satellites.

RAYMOND. Oh, I'm telling you *what* – you got one of *those* things – a vehicle like *that*? You're going across the country, driving here and there, looking at this and that, you feel like stopping – what the hell? – you pull over, pop a cold one, turn on the toob – huh?

KENNY. Yeah.

RAYMOND. *Oh* yeah!

(A beat then…)

KENNY. Oh – jeez-o-beezus! Almost forgot. *(**KENNY** clears his throat then, sings…)* "Happy Birthday to you. Happy Birthday to you. Happy Birthday dear Ray-mond. Happy Birthday to you."

*(A beat. As **RAY** stares at the smiling **KENNY**. Finally…)*

RAYMOND. *What?*

KENNY. Yeah. Company newsletter. You know. Happy Birthday.

RAYMOND. It's tomorrow.

KENNY. What?

RAYMOND. They're wrong. It's tomorrow.

KENNY. Oh. Well…anyway. You know.

(beat)

RAYMOND. Yeah, well…Thanks. Thanks. Yeah. 47. Forty… *(a depressed beat)* Seven.

KENNY. Wow.

RAYMOND. 47.

(This has brought him down. A beat, then, a morose sigh.)

KENNY. What?

*(**RAYMOND** continues to muse.)*

Hey, Raymond –

RAYMOND. *(coming to)* Huh?

KENNY. You O.K.?

RAYMOND. Oh. Yeah…yeah. I just…

(dismissing it with a laugh)

Ah, hell, I don't know, Kenny. I don't know.

KENNY. *(as if understanding.)* Ohhh.

*(**KENNY** takes a bite of his sandwich as **RAY** watches. Then, contentedly…)*

This is a great sandwich.

RAYMOND. What you got?

KENNY. Peanut butter.

RAYMOND. Peanut butter? *(**KENNY** nods.)* Peanut butter and what?

KENNY. Peanut butter and nothin.

RAYMOND. You're kidding.

KENNY. Great sandwich.

RAYMOND. It's peanut butter.

KENNY. *(happily)* Yeah.

RAYMOND. It's a peanut butter sandwich, Kenny. How great can it be?

*(**KENNY** shrugs. A beat then…)*

KENNY. This is very good.

RAYMOND. See, Kenny, *that's* the difference.

KENNY. Between us?

RAYMOND. Between us – exactly.

KENNY. *(shrugging)* I like what I like.

*(A beat. As **RAY** contemplates this. Then…)*

RAYMOND. So, I don't know. Maybe I'll go fishing or something.

KENNY. You like to fish, Raymond?

RAYMOND. Oh…well, now, hey – see, fishing, Kenny, *fishing* –

KENNY. Yeah?

RAYMOND. *(enthusiastically)* Are you kidding me? Out on some pond or lake? Maybe a creek? You know what I'm saying?

KENNY. *(taking a bite of his sandwich)* Yeah?

RAYMOND. Yeah, see, Kenny, what you'd do is you'd get your…your thing, your – whaddayacallit – your… your –

KENNY. Pole – ?

RAYMOND. Yeah – a pole, Kenny. Sure – your *fishing* pole. And you'd get your little box – maybe so big – filled with hooks and string, maybe one of those little corks, perhaps a worm or two maybe, huh?

KENNY. *(taking a bite of his sandwich)* Bait.

RAYMOND. Bait, sure –

KENNY. Yeah.

RAYMOND. And then you'd…well, you know – you'd catch a fish. Maybe – I don't know – a trout maybe, huh?

KENNY. *(nodding and chewing)* Trout –

RAYMOND. Huh?

KENNY. Yeah.

RAYMOND. A trout, sure. *(a beat)* And the remarkable thing, Kenny, see – the *remarkable* thing – is you'd just sit there, not a care in the world, not thinking about nothing, no bullshit about it. You'd just sit there – catching trouts. *(Looking to the distance. Beat.)* Catching…trouts.

KENNY. I like to fish.

(beat)

RAYMOND. You do?

KENNY. I love to fish, Ray.

RAYMOND. Oh. *(beat)* Well, then…there you go!

KENNY. *(enthusiastically)* I didn't know you liked to fish! I mean – hey – we oughta go sometime, you know, the two of us? Some Saturday – we oughta pack a coupla sandwiches, take a six-pack, rent a boat? We oughta go some time, Ray.

RAYMOND. Yeah, well –

KENNY. We oughta!

RAYMOND. Sure – no question but, see, Kenny… I never actually been fishing in my life.

KENNY. Oh.

RAYMOND. Yeah, fact of the matter is…I don't know what the hell I'm talking about.

KENNY. But I thought –

RAYMOND. What I meant was maybe I'd do it *some* day. O.K.? *Some* day.

(KENNY muses. Then…)

KENNY. Ohhhh. *Some* day.

RAYMOND. Right. *(beat)* Yeah. Idn't that something? I live all this time, I never been fishing before.

KENNY. *(nodding, chewing, and musing)* Huh.

RAYMOND. Just never got around to it. Don't have a boat, you know. Or a pole. *(beat)* And, a course, it's pretty dangerous, idn't it?

KENNY. Dangerous?

RAYMOND. The water's…pretty deep, idn't it?

KENNY. I don't know. Sometimes.

RAYMOND. Yeah. Cause, see, I don't actually swim either.

KENNY. Oh.

RAYMOND. But I got plans, Kenny, don't get me wrong. It's on my list. Definitely on the lista things I gotta get round to. That and maybe gettin me a truck. You know – with one of those tops.

KENNY. *(simultaneously)* – one of those tops. Yeah.

RAYMOND. Absolutely! Oh, Kenny, hitting the road? Gettin the hell outta *here*? Huh?

KENNY. Yeah?

RAYMOND. The road calls to me, Kenny, honest to God, like a voice singin out loud and clear it calls to me.

*(Beat. As **RAY** ponders. A grunt.)*

Huh.

KENNY. What, Ray?

RAYMOND. *(A deep breath as he collects himself.)* The most, Kenny – the *most* curious things been happenin to me lately one after the other – Boom-boom-boom – I mean... *(beat)* The strangest thing, the strangest thing... other day, O.K.? Other day Tommy Rossiter – you know the guy with the goofy eye lives over on Water Street?

KENNY. Yeah?

RAYMOND. He gives me a lift out to the Wal-Mart in that crappy Oldsmobile he's got and we're on the bypass when – pow – we blow a tire! And *Tommy* – he doesn't have a spare, the car's such a piece a shit, so he keeps drivin, you know, till he can get to Wal-Mart and maybe, I don't know, steal one or something, the worthless son of a bitch.

(He takes a bite of sandwich.)

KENNY. *(grunting in agreement)* Huh.

RAYMOND. Anyhow...we're goin maybe 20 miles a hour, the tire's flappin, Tommy's screaming at the top of his lungs he's so pissed, all the time that goofy eyeball of his is rolling around in his head like a marble or something –

KENNY. He's a scary guy –

RAYMOND. Oh, he's a frightening individual. Anyhow, I'm sittin there – I'm miserable, Kenny, miserable – and I say to myself "Well, your life's come down to this, asshole – you're in this crappy car goin 20 miles a hour to nowhere with crazy goofy-eyed Tommy Rossiter!" It was a nightmare, boy. A nightmare! Depressed the hell outta me, Kenny.

KENNY. *(chewing and shaking his head)* Huh.

RAYMOND. *Really* brought me down. I mean, the whole time, I'm listenin to this flat slap the road – "Flap-te-flap, flap-te-flap, flap-te-flap" over and over and over. But *then* – and here's the curious part, Kenny – after a while, it starts sounding different. It starts sounding like this, it starts sounding like "Fet-ter-man, Fet-ter-man, Fet-ter-man." See? "Fet-ter-man, Fet-ter-man" – Huh?

KENNY. *(grunting and chewing)* Wow.

RAYMOND. You hear *that?*

KENNY. Wow.

RAYMOND. It was calling me! The road was actually calling me! I couldn't believe something so magical was happening to me, Kenny, and I go, like, "Whoa, ho, I hear *that*, boy, I hear that loud and clear, you don't gotta call me two times, and just as soon as I'm outta this crappy Oldsmobile...?" *(beat)* I mean, it was just this curious event but it put me in the mind, Kenny, in the mind, boy. I mean – *(A "zooming" motion.)* Zoom! You know? Huh?

(Beat. As **RAY** *chews and thinks:)*

Yeah. Yeah, a truck would be pretty good.

KENNY. A truck would be great.

RAYMOND. A truck would be *terrific*! One of those little tops, a TV inside, a coupla six-packs, and a full tanka gas? Kenny – my God! A man – listen to me, Kenny – a man with such a vehicle could drive many miles from *here*, I wanna tell you! Many miles. *(Beat. As he nods, looking off.)* "Fet-ter-man, Fet-ter-man...Fet-ter-man." *(beat)* Give me a truck and I could be going somewhere, I'll tell you that right now. Some day, Frankly? Some day.

*(***KENNY*** muses. Then, pulls a picture from his pocket.)*

KENNY. Oh, hey. Lookit.

(He hands **RAYMOND** *the picture. Then...)*

RAYMOND. What's this – your kid?

KENNY. Yeah – that's my little girl, Raymond. That's Shelby.

RAYMOND. Boy, she's shootin up there, idn't she?

*(***KENNY*** nods.)*

Lookit that smile! Kenny – and those *eyes?* Huh?

KENNY. Yeah. *(Beat. Then an explanation.)* Just got the picture.

RAYMOND. Oh, she's a heartbreaker *this* one, I wanna tell you!

KENNY. I think she kinda looks like her mom. That's what everybody says, at least. I don't know. *(beat)* She's 8 now.

RAYMOND. What is she – in a bunch of colored *balls*?

(KENNY nods.)

Why she in balls?

KENNY. McDonalds. That's where I took the picture. They got this little room with colored balls kids can jump in – so long as you take your shoes off. She loves it.

RAYMOND. *(still looking at the picture)* Who wouldn't?

KENNY. Yeah. She's in the third grade now. She did good in second but *this* year – ? Jeez-o-beezus. She's having a real hard time with math.

(RAY looks at KENNY. Then, answering him...)

Negatives.

RAYMOND. *What?*

KENNY. I tried to help her but me and math – oh boy! I'm o.k. with the positives, adding I can do, some dividin, maybe, you know, but when you start talkin negatives to me – I mean, oh boy!

RAYMOND. Whaddya mean negatives?

KENNY. Numbers. Negative numbers. Numbers that aren't there. Fact, numbers that are *less* than not there. Figure *that* out, boy. How can you have something that's less than not there?

(Pause. The question seems to have depressed RAYMOND.)

RAYMOND. *(with a sigh)* Ah, shit…Biggest mystery in my life I don't have 3 maybe 4 tykes runnin' around saying "Daddy do this" and "Daddy do that" and "Daddy buy me this…this…item or other." *(a sigh)* I wanna tell you what – this… *(holding up picture)* this right here has always been *my* dream.

KENNY. *(with a surprised laugh)* *What?*

RAYMOND. Yeah.

KENNY. You're kidding –

RAYMOND. No.

KENNY. *(with a smile)* Since *when?*

RAYMOND. Since always.

KENNY. *(with a dubious shrug)* O.K.

RAYMOND. No, to have some *youngsters?* Hey, listen – what else is there? I mean, really – Kenny – you're a family man. You know what I'm saying – what else is there?

*(Beat. As **RAYMOND** looks at the picture. Then...)*

I don't know, Kenny. I don't know.

*(He hands **KENNY** the picture.)*

KENNY. Hey, Raymond – what about Rachel? You been goin out I bet maybe a coupla times a week for awhile now. Right? Maybe you and Rachel...

RAYMOND. What?

KENNY. You know.

RAYMOND. Ah, well, see, Rachel, Kenny...Rach...

KENNY. What?

RAYMOND. Lately – and I don't know why even though I keep asking her – but *lately* I been getting the idea she's maybe less than happy with the idea of me and her, you know?

KENNY. *(realization)* Ohhhh....

RAYMOND. See – she's been givin me these looks, Kenny. Outta the corner of my eye, I catch her looking at me with this look that says "Jesus Christ, what the hell was I thinking?"

KENNY. *(helpfully)* Maybe she's just tired.

(beat)

RAYMOND. What?

KENNY. She's workin a couple of jobs, right?

*(**RAYMOND** nods.)*

Well, then, there you go.

RAYMOND. Maybe she's *tired?*

KENNY. Sure. Whenever I get tired people always look at me like I'm looking at them.

(a confused little pause)

RAYMOND. What the hell are you talking about, Kenny?

KENNY. Well, O.K. Coupla years ago? When I was working at that warehouse? There was this one time. Jeez-o-beezus...things had been pretty bad, boy. You know? Pretty bad. We needed the money and...and I needed to stay busy anyway 'cause of...cause of things.

(Frowning, he muses a moment. Then, upbeat again...)

Anyhow, I'd pulled something like maybe five double shifts in a row and I was tired, boy. I mean, I was *really* tired.

(licks some errant peanut butter off a finger)

Mmm....

(KENNY *wipes crumbs off his shirt and* **RAY** *watches with a certain fascinated irritation.)*

So. Anyhow – I pop into Nate's on the way home from work this one night – you know, just to try and relax before I had to go home – and I'm sitting there, having a beer, minding my own beeswax, just starin' like you do when you're really tired, you know, just starin' like this – *(He stares.)* – you know, cause I was so tired? And this guy walks up and – *(a "1-2" punch at an invisible jaw)* BAM-A-DA, BAM-A-DA! Knocks the crap outta me so hard I start to cry. I say "Jeez-o-beezus why did you do that?" He says "Stop starin' at me!" And I said "I'm not starin' at you. I'm just tired." And he goes, "Oh." **(KENNY** *shrugs.)* We had a pretty good laugh about it.

(Beat. Then...)

RAYMOND. The guy beats the crap outta you and you had a good laugh about it?

*(**KENNY** considers this. Then...)*

KENNY. *(shrugging)* I dunno....Anyway, so maybe that's

probably all it is with Rachel. You know – with the looks and everything.

RAYMOND. So, what you're saying is – ?

KENNY. It's probably a misunderstanding – sure.

RAYMOND. You think?

KENNY. What else could it be? I mean, she told me she thought you were O.K.

RAYMOND. Get outta here –

KENNY. No, Ray, I talked to her that one time – ?

RAYMOND. Yeah?

KENNY. Company picnic?

RAYMOND. Yeah?

KENNY. She said you were O.K.

(beat)

RAYMOND. She said that?

(KENNY nods.)

Huh. Well...

(RAYMOND considers this for a moment. Beat.)

So tell me something – you and the wife are...pretty close, right?

(Beat. Then KENNY shrugs...)

KENNY. She's my wife.

RAYMOND. Then there you go.

KENNY. There you go.

(beat)

RAYMOND. So...when did you...*know*, you know? When'd you *know*?

KENNY. What – you mean that she was – ?

RAYMOND. Yeah. You know.

KENNY. *(considering this)* Huh. *(Beat. Then, with a shrug...)* I don't know. I guess it was probably that one time I said "I love you" and she just said it back to me.

RAYMOND. Yeah?

(KENNY nods.)

Well, what about that, huh? See, that's great, Kenny. That's out*stand*ing. I wanna tell you *what*, that's…. that's… *(Beat. Then, a realization.)* Boy, that's curious.

KENNY. What?

RAYMOND. That is really a curious thing you should say that because, see, I started thinkin about this very thing the other day and, Kenny, it's a mystery to me. All this time we're together, Rachel…*(stopping, an embarrassed laugh)* Nevermind. This is nuts, this nonsense here. Forget it.

KENNY. What?

RAYMOND. Forget it –

KENNY. Come on –

RAYMOND. Nah –

KENNY. Ray – what?

(A beat then…)

RAYMOND. Well…alright. All this time we're together, Rachel's never said to me…"I love you." There. Idn't that something? Funny thing is, tell you the truth, this used to never mean nothing to me I hear this or not, you know? I didn't care. Hey – *(confidentially.)* To *me*, you only said that when you *wanted* something…if you know what I'm talking about, right?

KENNY. *(modding)* Yeah.

RAYMOND. Absolutely. But lately, Kenny, lately… *(Beat. Then, rather amazed…)* I've said it to Rachel, boy, 3 maybe 4 times – and not because I was trying to get something, y'know?

KENNY. Yeah.

RAYMOND. Yeah. But nothin', Kenny. Not even a rebound. Not even a "same to you" or "right back at you." *Nothin'.*

KENNY. Oh.

RAYMOND. I mean, there was this one time I *thought* maybe she said it but… *(beat)* O.K. See, this one night we're at Eat 'n Park, we're havin the wings, you know? And we were actually having a good time! So she leans over for some reason and she says something that I didn't catch – she had a buncha potato salad in her mouth – but I *thought* she said – "I love you, Ray." *(beat)* Oh, I wanna tell you *what*, Kenny – knocked me on my ass, I was so surprised to hear this but, see, I wasn't sure, right? Cause of the potato salad, you know. So I said "What's that I hear, Rach? What's *that*, huh? You say what I *think* you said? You say to me "I love you?" And she looked at me like the way I was tellin you about and said "What're you – nuts?" *(Beat. An embarrassed laugh.)* I don't know. Maybe it's enough for her we go out, we get along O.K., we maybe fool around every now and then she feels up to it. Maybe it's enough for her we just share some laughs, some chuckles, you know, the way you do when you get used to each other. But for me? *(beat)* I gotta be honest with you, Kenny – and don't tell nobody this or, I swear, I'll beat the shit outta you –

KENNY. I won't.

RAYMOND. It dawns on me the other day that I'm this far from being 47 years old? My whole life I never had nobody ever say this to me. Can you imagine such a thing? You hear about it in songs, they say it all the time on TV. I see people walkin around together – I know they gotta be saying it to each other all the time. You can tell just by lookin at them. And I wonder, Kenny. I wonder sometimes just what it's gotta be like to have somebody say this phrase to you. I wonder how long I gotta wait cause – truth be known, Kenny? I think I'm at the point in my life when I gotta know I ain't facing it all alone.

(Beat. As **KENNY** *considers this.)*

KENNY. Sometimes it takes a while to figure out you're supposed to be with somebody.

(beat)

RAYMOND. You think?

KENNY. Like I said – she told me she thought you were O.K. that one time.

(beat)

RAYMOND. So she actually *said* that? Coupla weeks ago? Company picnic?

*(**KENNY** nods and **RAY** thinks. Then…)*

Well, Kenny, you know, I hope so. Honest to God, I hope so so hard I don't know *what*. 'Cause, see, Rach – from the first time I laid eyes on her – I am not shitting you in this regard Kenny –

KENNY. Yeah?

RAYMOND. See, she's got this smile, Kenny, this *smile*, you know?

KENNY. *Rachel?*

RAYMOND. You kidding *me?* Kenny, my God…!

*(**RAY** is speechless for once.)*

KENNY. Jeez-o-beezus. I can't remember ever even seeing her smile.

RAYMOND. Well… she doesn't too much. See, she's had these things, Kenny, these sad and tragic things in her life. But when she *does*, Kenny? When she smiles this *smile?*

(beat)

KENNY. *(sincerely)* That's great, Ray.

RAYMOND. *(enthusiastically)* No question of it – I can turn it around, I can turn it *right* around! Oh, boy, I wanna tell you what, Kenny – me and Rach? A truck with a microwave and a *crapper?*

KENNY. Yeah?

RAYMOND. A coupla tykes?

KENNY. Yeah?

RAYMOND. What – are you shitting me? Life, Kenny…?

KENNY. Yeah?

RAYMOND. Life is full of endless possibilities!

KENNY. Yeah.

(RAYMOND muses and KENNY pulls a cellophane wrapped snack cake from his lunch box.)

Wanna split this Moon Pie?

(beat)

RAYMOND. A *Moon* Pie?

KENNY. Yeah – it's got marshmallow squooshed up inside and chocolate and –

RAYMOND. I know what a Moon Pie is, Kenny.

KENNY. *(holding out the moon pie)* You want?

(RAYMOND shakes his head.)

These aren't Moon Pies. They're called something else. But they're really Moon Pies. You know. *(KENNY unwraps the Moon Pie.)* I eat 3 or 4 a day, boy. They're great. *(takes a bite)* I eat'em all the time. Like, a lotta times I have a hard time sleeping? I mean, I can *get* to sleep – I just wake up. You know. Sometimes. So... when I wake up? Eat a Moon Pie.

(Nods and chews. RAYMOND watches KENNY luxuriate.)

RAYMOND. So – does it work?

KENNY. *(chewing)* Huh?

RAYMOND. The Moon Pie. It put you to sleep?

KENNY. Oh. No. *(little laugh)* No. When I wake up I usually stay up. A Moon Pie just makes it easier to be awake. Makes me feel better for a little while at least. I mean, I'll wake up and...lie there and think. Then I get up and go to the kitchen so I don't wake up Gail cause – you know...she's got to get to work early and get the kids off.

(takes a bite)

RAYMOND. Kids? *(beat)*

KENNY. Huh?

RAYMOND. *Kids?* You said "kids."

(A beat. Then...)

KENNY. Oh! *(a little laugh)* No. I mean, Shelby. *(beat)* Just Shelby.

*(Pause as a suddenly pensive **KENNY** savors his Moon Pie.)*

Sometimes I go out on the stoop, eat me a Moon Pie, just sorta sit til I get calmed down. Look at the night, you know. This one time I was lookin at the sky and I saw the moon and I started to laugh cause I was eatin a Moon Pie, staring at the moon. Get it? *(A little laugh.)* I thought it was pretty funny. Eatin a Moon Pie, staring at the moon. *(Beat. Then, musing...)* That could be a song or something. *(Takes a bite of his Moon Pie.)* This is great.

*(Beat. As **RAYMOND** looks intently at **KENNY**. Then...)*

RAYMOND. *(with a soft laugh)* Ah, Kenny –

KENNY. What, Ray?

RAYMOND. You, boy. *You...*

KENNY. Yeah?

RAYMOND. I wanna tell you what – you got a wife, you got a tyke...you go *fishing? You* gotta a life, boy. You gotta a life.

(a beat)

KENNY. *(softly)* Yeah...I guess.

RAYMOND. And, hey, Kenny – who knows? Right? *(enumerating on his fingers)* I get me a truck, I take Rachel, we hit the road, I do me some fishing and raise a coupla *tykes? That* would be a life! Right? Huh?

(A beat. Then, quietly...)

Yeah...That would be a life.

*(**KENNY** muses for a moment, then stands and stretches.)*

KENNY. Well...better get started.

(**KENNY** *throws garbage away.*)

RAYMOND. What? What're you doin?

KENNY. You know – gettin back to work. You know.

RAYMOND. *(groaning)* I wanna tell you *what* – biggest shock a my life I gotta take orders from people of this quality.

KENNY. *(crossing to boxes)* Yeah.

RAYMOND. I mean, c'mon, Kenny – *this*...this is just nonsense here, that's what this is with the boxes.

KENNY. *(picking up a box and carrying it to the other side)* Yeah. Boy.

RAYMOND. *(as he walks toward the boxes)* Grippo thinks I'm shoving about *these* things...?

KENNY. It's just boxes –

RAYMOND. Boxes with *stuff*!

(**RAY** *is trying to open a small box by picking at the tape.*)

KENNY. Hey, come on, Ray! Don't do that –

RAYMOND. *(roughly shaking the box)* What's in these things I wonder?

KENNY. *(crossing with a box)* Who cares?

RAYMOND. This doesn't concern you?

KENNY. No.

RAYMOND. This doesn't bother you?

KENNY. No.

RAYMOND. See, this is the difference.

KENNY. *(crossing back to the stack)* Between us?

RAYMOND. Between us – exactly.

KENNY. Ray, the company's paying me –

(pushes a large box a few feet)

9.50 a hour –

(pushes the box a bit more)

to do what the suits tell me to do.

(Pushes again. Then...)

Grippo says we gotta move boxes, I'm gonna move boxes.

(pushes the rest of the way to the other side. Then...)

I don't care why, I don't care what – I need this job. I gotta move boxes cause I got people depending on me. That's all the reason I need. That's all. I gotta family.

(beat)

RAYMOND. Oh. And I don't, right? Is that what you're saying?

KENNY. *(a bit flustered)* Well...yeah, but...I mean, no. No, that's not what I –

RAYMOND. *(with an edge)* Hey – no, Kenny. You're right. Sure. You're a fortunate man. No question. A very fortunate man.

(beat)

KENNY. Look...I'm sorry. Just...Grippo said to get this done so let's just get this done. O.K.? It's just moving boxes. It's no biggie.

*(**KENNY** picks up a box.)*

O.K.?

(beat)

O.K.?

*(A pause. Finally, **RAY** crosses to the stack, muttering.)*

RAYMOND. I gotta hernia or something, maybe something twisted in my spine or something. I'm in a certain amount of discomfort here. I wanna tell you *what...* I think maybe I'm looking at some kinda legal action, boy.

*(**RAY** picks up the smallest box he can find and meanders over towards the other side. He drops the box. Then...)*

Lookit this. *(beat)* You ever in your life think you'd be moving boxes for a living? Boxes, Kenny, boxes? I mean, no, really – you ever think it would come to this?

*(**RAYMOND** has stopped again and watches **KENNY***

work.)

KENNY. I never thought of it like that.

RAYMOND. So what'd you wanna do when you're a youngster?

KENNY. *(wearily)* I don't know, Ray –

RAYMOND. No – come on. Really. What?

KENNY. *(picking up a box)* Ray –

RAYMOND. I wanna talk, O.K.? We'll move the goddamn boxes but I just wanna talk! Pass the time while we work. That O.K. by you?

(KENNY shrugs, thinks a moment. Then...)

KENNY. A elevator operator.

RAYMOND. What?

KENNY. I used to wanna be a elevator operator.

(KENNY crosses back.)

RAYMOND. An elevator operator?

KENNY. When I was a kid.

RAYMOND. Your dream was to become an elevator operator?

KENNY. I guess so. Yeah.

RAYMOND. Kenny – I don't think they even *have* those guys anymore.

(KENNY puts the box down.)

KENNY. But they *used* to. Jeez-o-beezus, I thought it would be great. Get to ride in a elevator all day. Wear a neat little uniform like they do. Open the doors for people, ask'em what floor they want, if they were havin a good day, ask'em "How 'bout them Pirates?" push the button, and just ride up and down. All day. I always thought that would be a great job.

(Beat. As **RAYMOND** *considers this. Then...)*

RAYMOND. Well, then, there you go.

KENNY. There you go.

RAYMOND. You aspired to other things. Moving boxes? You

know where that job is on my all-time list of things to do? About number 2000.

(**RAYMOND** *muses as* **KENNY** *picks up another good-sized box.*)

KENNY. What about you?

RAYMOND. Huh?

KENNY. You ever think you'd be doing this?

RAYMOND. I did *not.*

KENNY. What did you want to do?

(*Long pause as* **RAY** *thinks. Finally, giving up...*)

RAYMOND. Not this. *(beat)* Not this.

(*Pause.* **KENNY** *picks up a large box by himself.* **RAYMOND** *pushes a small box along the floor with his foot. Finally...*)

Ten years I been workin here and as far as Grippo and the suits are concerned, I'm nothing more than one of those boxes, just something to get shoved around whenever they feel like it.

(**RAY** *stands, thinking. Then...*)

KENNY. Hey, Raymond...? Ray?

RAYMOND. *(with a soft laugh)* Ah, shit...let me tell you something about dreams. More and more I wonder if dreams aren't nothing but these things that happen to you when you're unconscious.

(beat)

KENNY. Jeez-o-beezus, Ray, you O.K.?

RAYMOND. Huh?

KENNY. You been kinda...I don't know – *different* or something, you know?

RAYMOND. So you noticed this about me too, huh?

KENNY. I just never heard you talk about stuff like you been talkin about stuff. I mean...you O.K.?

RAYMOND. Am I O.K.? *(A beat. As he sits.)* Kenny – I got a crappy job, I gotta crappy room in a crappy boarding house, I gotta girlfriend givin' me looks, these...these *looks*. I'm 47 minus one day – 40 damn 7 – and on top of all that *shit*, guess, Kenny – just guess how old my old man was when he died. Huh? Go on, Kenny, go on – give it a try. Just how old you suppose my old man was when he croaked?

KENNY. 47?

RAYMOND. No...he was 49.

KENNY. Oh.

RAYMOND. But still, though, *still*. Huh? 47? The clock is ticking, Kenny, it's *ticking*. Lately I been thinkin about this and thinkin about this and I'm thinkin some day, boy, maybe sooner than later – but some day...? *(Beat.)* I wanna tell you *what*, Kenny –

KENNY. *(with a weary sigh)* What, Ray?

RAYMOND. Other night – last Thursday...

*(Beat. **KENNY** continues to work.)*

Oh, this is curious, Kenny – this is very curious...

*(A beat. As **RAY** "collects" himself.)*

I'm down at Stinky Tucker's with this buddy of mine who lives around the corner from me – Billy Hudak, works for PennDot, married to that chick works at the Zippy Mart – doesn't matter. Anyhow...we're throwing darts like always, listening to the Pirates on the radio – they're playing the Reds – doesn't matter – and we're pounding them back – 1, 2, 3 – when this geezer walks over to us –

KENNY. Who?

RAYMOND. Doesn't matter – just some old guy. I don't know. Seen him around for years. Used to hang out with that other old guy Leo works down in shipping and receiving –

KENNY. Oh, yeah – !

RAYMOND. Right. Anyway, Kenny – point is –

KENNY. I know *him*.

RAYMOND. Yeah, right, whatever but listen, Kenny –

KENNY. Walt. His name is Walt!

RAYMOND. Walt, yeah, right, fine, whatever, Jesus *Christ*! The point is, Kenny, the point is…*(another deep breath)* What happened was this old guy Walt comes over, he starts talkin to me and Billy about the Pirates and how he used go with his buddy Leo and see Clemente play and Stargell play and how the game has changed – you know – geezer talk. And I'm lettin him go on and on, you know, cause he's this old guy when – I'm not shitting you in this regard – he gets these tears in his eyes and, outta the blue, he starts talking about his life and…and he starts talkin all this nonsense, all this philosophy. This…this – *philosophy*, right? Sayin all these things, thinkin all these thoughts and before you know it, I find myself listenin to the geezer, tryin real hard to figure out why – all of sudden – he's gotta pick on me to talk to. Why me? Now, by this time, the geezer's on a first name basis with me saying things like, "Whaddya think, Ray?" and "What's your take on that, Ray?" "Whaddya say to *that*, Ray?" and, hell, I didn't know, Kenny, I didn't know and I tell him this I say "I don't know – I never think about stuff" and he – now get *this*, Kenny – he shakes his head, slaps me on the shoulder and says "Ray, you need to live in a bigger world, kid. Don't let nobody tell you any different." Then…he finishes his beer, looks me straight in the eye with this kinda sad little smile, and says "Well, guess that's it." I thought that was very curious thing to say at the time but I figured – what the hell – he's a geezer. So he walks outta Stinky Tucker's without another word, goes straight down the street to where he hangs out with old Leo and these other pals of his…?

KENNY. Yeah?

RAYMOND. Drops dead.

(beat)

KENNY. What?

RAYMOND. Checks out. Bingo. Ticker. Maybe a stroke. They don't know.

KENNY. *(softly)* Wow.

(Beat. As he begins to move a box.)

RAYMOND. Don't you see?

KENNY. *(crossing)* No.

RAYMOND. He knew, Kenny! He knew!

KENNY. *(setting box down)* Oh.

RAYMOND. *(persisting)* Said "That's it" and checks out. "That's *it*?" What else could he have meant? I mean, Kenny, the geezer musta saw his own death! He had a...a vision. He had – no question of it – a vision.

KENNY. Oh.

RAYMOND. Huh? Idn't that the spookiest thing you ever heard? All of a sudden you know beyond a shadow of a doubt that in the next coupla minutes you're gonna croak? You ever in your life hear such a thing?

(KENNY picks up a box.)

KENNY. I had a aunt one time could tell when it was goin to rain. *(Beat. Then, an explanation...)* 'Cause a her knee.

RAYMOND. That's not the same thing!

(KENNY crosses toward the other side.)

KENNY. I know, Ray. I know. I just...I wanna move these boxes, O.K.?

RAYMOND. But, Kenny, the thing is – the spookiest, most mysterious thing of *all* is – I was looking him in the eyes, right in the eyes when he said this to me and what I saw in his eyes, Kenny, I been seeing in the mirror every day since he croaked. Every morning I been seeing that same geezer look, lookin back at me, making me wonder, Kenny, am I having the same vision the geezer had? Is today the day? Am I lookin' at a dead man by the end of the day?

KENNY. *(wearily)* Ray, visions aren't contagious.

RAYMOND. I don't know that! How else I explain what I been feeling lately?

KENNY. I don't know –

RAYMOND. *(pressing* **KENNY***)* How else I explain these curious events?

KENNY. I told you –

RAYMOND. How else I explain these feelings that things just ain't right?

KENNY. *(grabbing another box)* I don't like thinking about this, Ray!

RAYMOND. Who does? I *hate* thinking, Kenny, you know this about me! I hate thinking these things I been thinking! *(beat)* Goddamnit! Five days…Kenny – five days ago I didn't have a thought in my head and my life was a wondrous thing to behold. I had three hots and a flop, I did what I wanted, when I wanted – didn't answer to nobody, didn't question nothing. I had a circle of pals and associates I shared more than a few chuckles with and maybe, if I'm lucky, a coupla times a week I lose myself for a moment with Rach. All was right with the world. I did not want, Kenny. And then… *(A beat. Struggling.)* And then, outta nowhere – Wham! – the geezer has his horrible vision, he croaks, and next thing I know, all these *events*, Kenny, these curious, curious events start happening, all these…these things and feelings coming together the last few days, making me think things I don't wanna think, making me realize things I don't wanna realize, making me ask these questions, these…these goddamn questions that got no answers. *(beat)* No…no – it's ticking, boy, it's ticking…and I got nothing to show for it. You talk about your kid with the negatives? I'm *livin'* the negatives, boy, 'cause I can't see nothin' beyond here and this.

(A pause. **KENNY** *uncomfortably looks from* **RAY** *to the boxes. Finally…)*

KENNY. Ray…we gotta get this done.

(Beat. As **RAY** *looks at* **KENNY***.)*

Look – I told you I don't like thinking about this! Now come on. Please?

(beat)

RAYMOND. *(softly)* Shit. That...see, *that's* the difference right there. That's the difference.

KENNY. Between us?

RAYMOND. Between us, exactly. You don't know what the hell I'm talking about, do you?

KENNY. I know.

RAYMOND. *(accusing)* No, you're just a *kid.* You don't gotta clue!

KENNY. I gotta clue, Ray!

RAYMOND. You don't gotta clue! You shove worthless shit around for no reason other than some suits tell you to and then you say "Oh, hey, Jeez-o-beezus – lookit me! I got 9.50 a hour, I gotta peanut butter sandwich, I gotta Moon Pie! I gotta tyke! Jeez-o-beezus! This is the life!"

KENNY. That's not true –

RAYMOND. What the hell was I expecting talking to you about these things? You don't know –

KENNY. I know –

RAYMOND. You don't know! You got no idea how fast your life can become nothing but this thing that happens while you pass the time. Me? I wanna tell you *what* – I bust my ass, I live my life, I do what you're supposed to do, all of a sudden, I turn around, I'm this far from 47 and I got nothing to show for it! Nothin', Kenny. *(beat)* So *that's* the difference. I don't have nothin and *you* don't know nothin about having nothin. You don't know.

KENNY. *(quietly)* I know if you got a lot you got more to lose.

RAYMOND. *(sarcastically)* Oh, Jesus Christ – *what?* You think I don't know *that?*

KENNY. I used to have two. *(beat)* Two kids. *(Answering* **RAYMOND***'s look.)* I ran over one.

(softly)

It was a accident. I didn't mean to but...

(Pause. Finally...)

RAYMOND. *(stunned) What?*

*(As **KENNY** speaks he continues to methodically move boxes.)*

KENNY. My little boy. Tony. He was 4. He always liked to watch when I worked on the car out in fronta the house. This one time I... *(a short laugh)* It was funny – he was running around wearing this old wig of Gail's? *(another little laugh)* He was a pretty funny little kid, boy. And he had this kinda stick he was using like it was – I don't know – like it was this gun? And he'd shoot cars, you know, when they drove by. This little boy with this long, curly, black wig with this stick shootin everybody. *(beat)* It was pretty funny. And every once in awhile he'd run up to me and shoot me. And sometimes I'd sorta pretend to fall over – you know like you do. Sometimes. Just playing with him. You know. But this one time, though...

(He stops moving boxes. This is difficult and he responds with a soft laugh.)

Oh man... *(beat)* This one time I told him to quit botherin me. Kinda yelled at him. You know – the way you do. And he said... *(beat)* He said "Jeez-o-beezus" – you know, cause he heard his ole man say it so much – "Jeez-o-beezus, Daddy." And he went off. I thought he went inside to his mamma. But he didn't and a little while later I had to go get something and I backed up... *(beat)* And I heard this bump. First thing I saw when I got outta the car was this black, curly wig so I knew what musta happened. *(Beat. A shrug.)* I looked but he was short. Anyway...there was nothin' I could do. The cops came in a little while, asked me all these questions. I'm standin there, lookin' at this wig. And this little spot of blood. That was all. Just... *(beat)* Cops didn't do nothin' to me. You know. Guess they figured I'd suffered enough. I had....I did....I do. *(beat)* 'Bout to a killed Gail. Boy, she was pretty pissed at me! Still is I think.

(an awkward little laugh)

Talk about gettin looks. *(Beat. Then, quietly.)* I know about havin nothin, Ray. I know *a lot* about havin nothin, O.K.? So, see, this? This ain't so bad, Ray. It's just movin boxes. That's all.

(KENNY Continues to move the boxes. Finally...)

RAYMOND. Shit, Kenny – you never said nothing to me before about runnin' over a kid.

KENNY. *(with a shrug)* It was 4 years ago – before I came here – when I was still workin over at that warehouse.

RAYMOND. But you never told me.

KENNY. I only known you a coupla months, Ray. You know.

RAYMOND. Why'd you never told me this before, Kenny?

KENNY. It's not something I like to talk about.

RAYMOND. I told you things about *my* life.

KENNY. *(not unkindly)* It's not a contest, Ray.

RAYMOND. But I thought we were...you know.

KENNY. It don't have nothin to do with you. I just don't talk about it. That's all. It don't mean we're not friends. I just...

RAYMOND. So...why you tell me now?

(Beat. Finally, with a shrug.)

KENNY. I wanted you to know I gotta clue, Ray. You said I didn't but I do. I mean, Jeez-o-beezus....We all get the shit kicked outta us every now and then. You, me, everybody. That's just the way it is. *(beat)* Now...can you give me a hand here? I need to keep busy.

(KENNY crosses to the boxes, picks one up, and crosses over to the other side. RAY is still struggling to make sense of what he's just heard. Finally...)

RAYMOND. I didn't know. I had no idea. That musta been... I don't know if it makes you feel any better but I've had people die on me too, you know.

(KENNY nods but continues.)

So, I kinda know what it's gotta feel like. I mean, I know it's not the same thing but....Is there anything

I can…?

(Beat. Finally, knowing nothing else to do…)

There, there.

(KENNY stops working.)

KENNY. What?

(RAY awkwardly pats KENNY on the shoulders.)

RAYMOND. There, there. *(KENNY is look ing at RAY. Beat.)* That's all I can say. It's stupid but…that's all I can say.

(RAYMOND crosses over to the boxes and sits down heavily, head in his hands. After a moment, KENNY crosses to sit beside RAYMOND. A long pause. Finally…)

KENNY. The preacher at Gail's church was this guy – this Mr. Latimer? He comes over to the house the day after it happened, you know. Jeez-o-beezus – it was real bad. Gail was kinda outta her mind. *(that soft, embarrassed laugh again)* It was real rough. This preacher tried to pray, he tried to talk to us. Mostly we just sorta…sat there. Finally, he mumbled something about it being God's will. And Gail…Jeez-o-beezus – Gail goes nuts. Tears into him. Screams "Why the hell would God want Kenny to drive over my little boy? You can't really believe that shit, do you?" And this guy Latimer – he gets this look on his face like he never thoughta that in his whole life and for the longest time he just… stared at us. Gail, boy – she's so pissed she goes outside with her mamma and has a smoke. I stayed. Sorta sat there. Didn't know what else to do. I wasn't feelin much of anything 'cept a lotta pain. You know. Boy. *(beat)* Then, all of a sudden… he starts to cry. Real quiet at first but then louder and louder. These great big sobs. Shoulders shakin up and down – the way they do when…when your heart's breaking? Jeez-o-beezus – I didn't know what to do so, finally, I get up, go in the kitchen, and get him a coke and a Moon Pie – you know, thinkin it might make him feel better. *(He laughs softly.)* I don't know – I guess you had to be there but it was kinda funny in that...kinda...*sad* kinda way. I'd just run over my little boy but I spent, I bet, maybe the next hour, you know, trying to make *him* feel better, the whole time he just kept crying and crying, saying "I'm sorry, I'm sorry, I'm sorry" over and over. So, finally, I sorta put my arm around his shoulders and said "There, there. There, there." And he looks at me? Jeez-o-beezus, Raymond...the guy was so grateful, you know? He was so grateful.

(Beat. This is a nice memory.)

Yeah. *(beat)* Yeah. Sometimes it's the only thing to say. You know –

*(He puts his hand on **RAYMOND**'s shoulder.)*

There, there?

RAYMOND. Yeah.

KENNY. There, there.

RAYMOND. *(with a heavy sigh)* Oh, yeah. Absolutely. Absolutely. No question. There, there.

KENNY. Yeah.

(A long pause as they are both lost in thought. Finally...)

RAYMOND. So....Boxes, huh?

KENNY. Yeah.

RAYMOND. Moving boxes...

KENNY. Back and forth.

RAYMOND. One side to the other.

(A pause. Then, finally, shaking his head...)

Damn.

*(They start to laugh and, the tension broken, **RAY** begins to move toward the boxes...)*

Alright – what the hell. No sense *both* our asses get canned.

KENNY. What?

*(**RAY** picks up a box. For a change, **KENNY** watches.)*

RAYMOND. Yeah. You believe this shit? On my way down here, Kenny, Grippo, O.K.? Grippo comes skippin up to me, wavin' that little notebook at me, says "There are issues, Fetterman, issues."

KENNY. "Issues?"

RAYMOND. Yeah. Says to me, says "There are *issues* Mr. Becker wants to talk to you about ASAP tomorrow A.M."

KENNY. Jeez-o-beezus.

(RAYMOND crosses back for another box.)

RAYMOND. "ASAP tomorrow A.M." Suits talk to you using letters you know it can't be good.

(A beat. As KENNY crosses to help.)

Ah…what the hell? I'm gonna be takin a different path anyway, Kenny. I mean, ten years? That's…that's a decade, that's what *that* is and I'm thinkin, lately, maybe what I need is a change. Yeah. I mean, I can't remember what I wanted to be when I was a youngster but I wanted to be *something* that wasn't *this*.

(He casually tosses a box onto the new stack.)

It's time, Kenny, you know? So this with Grippo – *this*… this is gonna be good.

(despite himself, without a great amount of conviction:)

Yeah. This is gonna be…this… *(softly)* Christ.

(A beat. As RAY is lost for a moment.)

KENNY. Well…Ray, you said the geezer told you that you needed to live in a bigger world. You know? Right?

(A beat. As RAY considers this.)

RAYMOND. Y'know, he *did* say that, Kenny.

KENNY. Yeah.

RAYMOND. *That* is a good point.

KENNY. *(picking up a box)* Sure.

RAYMOND. That is an *excellent* point. Oh, no question. No question at all – he was a very wise man, Kenny.

KENNY. Yeah.

RAYMOND. *(musing)* A very wise man.

(**KENNY** *nods and smiles at* **RAY**. *A beat. Then he picks up a box.* **RAY** *watches his friend for a moment and then, suddenly…*)

And, hey – at least he had the good fortune to croak with his chums, didn't he? I mean, he didn't have to go through it by himself, is what I'm saying.

KENNY. Yeah. I guess.

RAYMOND. Me? I wanna tell you *what* – the minute I start thinkin' about dropping dead, I'm gonna be poundin' the *shit* outta your door, boy!

(They both laugh. A beat. Then…)

O.K.?

KENNY. Huh?

RAYMOND. That O.K. I do that, Kenny?

(beat)

KENNY. *(sincerely)* Sure, Ray.

(A beat. Then, reassured, **RAY** *joins* **KENNY** *moving boxes.)*

RAYMOND. Yeah…yeah – you know, I'm thinking it's about time I get me that truck, Kenny.

KENNY. Great.

RAYMOND. So how much you think one of those things cost? With a camper top and a crapper and all.

KENNY. I dunno.

RAYMOND. Not as much as you'd think, I imagine.

KENNY. How much you got saved?

RAYMOND. $740.

(beat)

KENNY. Then there you go.

RAYMOND. There you go.

(They pick up the large box and start across the room. **RAY** *is, for the moment, upbeat. Again.)*

Oh, I wanna tell you what, Kenny – you live 47 years you learn one or two things – one or two lessons from life. Hey, listen – you're just this youngster, you probably don't know this but, Kenny – when I was a kid, there was this...this very great man. Somebody. A...a president I think. *Some*body. It's not important – anywho, he said something one time I'll never forget, Kenny, something very...very wise – something about "Ask..." *(Beat. Thinks.)* No... "Don't...?" *(thinks)* Yeah – "Don't ask people to do things for *you* but... just...do *something* for yourself" or something. Anyhow...these words of wisdom always stuck with me 'cause, you know, Kenny? They're true. You gotta make your own breaks in this world, boy, and, Kenny – I get me a *truck*? With a camper *top*? Headin' out on the open road, goin' back and forth, puttin' some miles between here and there, Kenny, between here and there? A truck would....see, I could just... a truck would be pretty great. *(beat)* Or a boat.

KENNY. What?

RAYMOND. I don't know. Maybe I'll get me a boat.

KENNY. Yeah?

RAYMOND. *Oh* yeah!

KENNY. A boat would be good.

RAYMOND. A boat would be *fantastic*! Adrift on the waves?

KENNY. That would be good.

RAYMOND. Catch a coupla fish now and then? Coupla trouts? Huh?

KENNY. Thought you didn't fish.

RAYMOND. Well, I would if I had a boat, Kenny. Give me a boat and I could catch me some fish. *(beat)* I wanna tell you *what* – that would be something, boy. *That* would be the life.

(They cross back to the stack and each pick up a box. They cross back and put them down are heading back as the lights fade out.)

End of Play

PROPERTY PLOT

GLENDA:
bowl of Doritos
paper napkin
2 drink glasses
water
soda
ice
tissues

WARREN:
pocket protector
handkerchief
assortment of ink pens
small wire-bound notebook
"Save-a-Bundle" name tag with "Warren, Assistant-Manager"
Tic-Tacs

KENNY:
lunch box
peanut butter sandwich in plastic baggie
Moon Pie *(in wrapper)*
canned soda
wallet
wallet-sized picture

RAYMOND:
paper lunch bag
sandwich in wax paper wrapping
canned soda

ONSTAGE
Act I
small sofa
coffee table
rocking chair
small bookcase
assortment of paperback romance novels
photo albums
"boom box"
small collection of CDs
"curio" cabinet
assortment of collectible figurines
magazines
framed "sampler" on the wall

Act II
Assorted OSHA "Safety First" posters
Bulletin board with paper memos attached
Small wooden crate
An assortment of mismatched folding chairs
20-30+ cardboard boxes of various sizes and weights
(Note: the more, the better!)
3-4 larger wooden crates

COSTUME PLOT

GLENDA:
Flower print dress
Sweater
"sensible" shoes

WARREN:
White short-sleeved dress shirt
Tie
Dark slacks
Black tie shoes

KENNY:
Dark work shirt w/ Save-a-Bundle patch and "Kenny" patch
Matching dark work pants
White tank-top t-shirt
Dirty tennis shoes

RAYMOND:
Dark work shirt w/ Save-a-Bundle patch and "Raymond" patch
Matching dark work pants
White t-shirt
White socks
Black work shoes

Also by
Ed Simpson...

The Battle of Shallowford

The Comet of St. Loomis

A Point of Order

Please visit our website **samuelfrench.com** for complete descriptions and licensing information

From the Reviews of
ADDITIONAL PARTICULARS...

"Los Angeles Drama Critics Circle Award" Winner
Backstage-West "Garland Award" Winner

"Critic's Choice" - *Los Angeles Times*
"Critic's Pick" - *Backstage West*

"...Human comedy par excellence, as if Chekhov were reincarnated in America's Wal-Mart culture...Simpson's sympathy and affection for (his character's) weaknesses are signs of that rare combination of a humanist with a genuine sense of humor."
- Robert Koehler, *Los Angeles Times*

"...Witty and insightful...not just a very funny show, but an unexpectedly poignant and decidedly human one as well.... Simpson writes with an unusual degree of humanity..."
- Terri Roberts, *Variety*

"...Poignantly funny...Full of angst and unfulfilled desires, Simpson's characters are heartbreakingly imperfect. Yet under the darkness, Simpson's works shine with an essential sweetness that is often a rarity in modern theater"
- F. Kathleen Foley, *Los Angeles Times*

"...Enchanting...delightfully funny and heartrending...With humor and despair always just a millisecond apart, Simpson's understated style aims squarely at the heart of working-class ennui and scores a bull's eye. This is a playwright worth watching."
- Les Spindle, *Backstage West*

"*Additional Particulars* triumphs....Written with down-to-earth humor and heartrending compassion...A peek at the heartland of America, this stunningly beautiful script captures the audience, and tugs at their heartstrings..."
- Pat Taylor, *The Tolucan Times*

"Big hearted...*Additional Particulars*...can easily join the ranks of those classic, timeless hymns to quiet humor and the human experience....The laughs are earned, not cheap. The tears are real, not manipulated."
- Mary Burkin, *The Burbank Leader*

Printed in the United States
205910BV00004B/568-639/P